Simply Pray

Simply Pray

A Modern Spiritual Practice to Deepen Your Life

Erik Walker Wikstrom

SKINNER HOUSE BOOKS
BOSTON

Cover design by Kathryn Sky-Peck.
Text design by Suzanne Morgan.
Printed in the United States.

ISBN 1-55896-469-X
978-1-55896-469-3

08 07
5 4 3 2

Library of Congress Cataloging-in-Publication Data

Wikstrom, Erik Walker.
   Simply pray : a modern spiritual practice to deepen your life / Erik Walker
Wikstrom.
      p. cm.
   Includes bibliographical references.
   ISBN 1-55896-469-X (alk. paper)
   1. Prayer. 2. Beads—Religious aspects. 3. Prayer—Christianity. I. Title.

BL560.W555 2005
204'.3—dc22
                                                        2004020934

We gratefully acknowledge:
Excerpt from "Little Gidding" in *Four Quartets*, copyright 1942 by T. S. Eliot and
renewed 1970 by Esme Valerie Eliot, reprinted by permission of Harcourt, Inc.
Excerpt from pp. 5-7 from *The Spiral Dance* by Starhawk, copyright 1979 by
Miriam Simos. Reprinted by permission of HarperCollins Publishers Inc.
Excerpt from *The Book of Secrets* by Osho. Copyright © 1998 by Osho and
reprinted by permission of St. Martin's Press, LLC.

For Rose Mary, Tilden, Dale, and Nancy,
and, of course, Mary, Theo, and Lester

Contents

Foreword

THOUGH I'VE BEEN a Unitarian Universalist for twenty years now, there remains in me the tiniest sliver of my Roman Catholic childhood, a fragment that most often emerges in spring. Throughout New York each May, on my way home from Sunday worship, I see the aftermath of First Communion Sunday—tiny girls in white lace dresses and little boys in crisp dark suits, all followed by happy parents holding small mementos of the day, including rosaries.

It's those rosaries that do it, of course. The strings of beads bring up a wealth of happy memories for me as a devout child, praying the Rosary each Friday in May. I loved the rhythmic quality of it, the sense of stillness and order I felt in the sanctuary of St. Ambrose, with my girlish prayers for peace joining those of others around the world. It's probably those memories—memories of the rightness of prayer, the sense of connection with God—that stayed with me long after I parted company with my childhood faith.

Decades later, prayer still matters to me. Unfortunately, my devotions seem to be the scattershot kind, mostly mumbled under my breath while I'm rushing to pick up my sons from school, or dashing to a church council meeting, or trying hard not to lose my temper. There are moments when I do better—lying in bed just before sleep, counting all my blessings to keep myself from worrying, and on Sunday mornings, just after I've preached, when I pray with and for the people I am privileged to serve as a parish minister. But what I miss, even after all these years, is that quiet, open, gracious feeling that used to greet me as I entered into the ritualized prayer of the Rosary. It was a feeling I imagined to be gone forever, the cost of my freedom from a religious community that no longer spoke to me. Erik Wikstrom, fortunately, has proven me wrong.

If prayer used to mean something to you but no longer does, *Simply Pray* might very well be the book that welcomes you home again. If prayer means little or nothing to you, I especially commend this book to you. At the very least, you will learn what it is that draws others to this form of spiritual practice, as well as how you might experiment with prayer on your own. All of us whose spirits seek communion with the Source of Life, whatever name we give it, can find one or more paths to follow in the course of reading this small volume.

The great gift of this book lies in its inclusive view of prayer. The roots of *Simply Pray* are in the Christian tradition, but its branches spread far, and readers of nearly every religious background will find both information and instruction that speak to their need. I am especially grateful for the author's tone—that of a friendly guide—which removes the last vestiges of guilt from spiritual practice, issuing instead a cordial welcome for every genuine seeker. Wikstrom doesn't assume what we know or don't know; he simply opens his ecumenical prayer book—and his heart—for our benefit. What we get, as a result, is a spiritual toolkit that many of us have longed for, right down to prayer beads and how to create them.

How good is *Simply Pray*? Good enough to read and reread; good enough to use as the basis of my next adult education class; good enough to send me to my local bead store, where I will start—bead by bead, prayer by precious prayer—to recreate a gracious center in my life again.

Rosemary Bray McNatt
December 2004

WHAT WE YEARN FOR

I HAVE GIVEN EACH BEING A SEPARATE AND UNIQUE WAY OF SEEING AND KNOWING AND SAYING THAT KNOWLEDGE. WHAT SEEMS WRONG TO YOU IS RIGHT FOR HIM. WHAT IS POISON TO ONE IS HONEY TO SOMEONE ELSE. PURITY AND IMPURITY, SLOTH AND DILIGENCE IN WORSHIP, THESE MEAN NOTHING TO ME. I AM APART FROM ALL THAT.

—RUMI

WHY DO PEOPLE PRAY? What does it bring to spirituality? Is there a "someone" or "something" that we encounter in our times of prayer, a "sacred something" that is yearning for relationship with us? Is prayer, as Anthony Bloom says, the building of a relationship or simply an internal monologue with one's own subconscious mind?

The Buddha's answer—"That is a question which does not tend toward edification"—is only a partial answer. The reason it does not "tend toward edification" is that it distracts our concentrated energy from the truly important task before us. We want to know with whom we are engaging—or whether or not there is a "whom"—before we will engage, yet to paraphrase Episcopal priest and author Martin Bell, "You cannot engage the sacred and then commit; commitment is the one and only way of engaging the sacred." To use another example, you can't find out what "wet" feels like unless you get into the water. There's simply no way to talk about it. There's no explaining it. There's no understanding it, even. There is only getting wet.

Similarly, you can't talk about a meal to someone and give them the taste of the food, or describe a symphony and expect them to experience the hearing of it; you can't explain what it feels like to run on the beach and hope that their muscles will know the feeling, or recite a poem about a rose with the intention that the hearer's nose will smell it. You can talk, describe, explain, and recite, of course, and doing these things will impart some measure of understanding. But in order for the other person to really know what you're talking about—deeply, fully—she or he will have to experience it directly. So it is with the spiritual journey. No words can truly describe it; you must experience it for yourself.

This is not the approach most people associate with "religion." Instead, after having been given a lot of concepts they are expected to understand—or at least memorize—people are often invited to fit their experiences into prefabricated cubby holes. This is what God is, they are told, now go and find him. This is what a spiritual experience feels like, now go and have one. For a lot of us this doesn't work too well—at some point we get stuck in the concepts, unable to see beyond them, and so we find nothing.

Not all religions are like this, however. In his interview with Bill Moyers, Joseph Campbell told the story of a Shinto priest who was attending an interfaith religious conference. Someone asked him if he could explain the Shinto theology or ideology. The priest thought for a moment and then replied, "We don't have a theology; we don't have an ideology. We dance."

There are other traditions like this, of course, that do not put such weight on the working of the mind, traditions that do not imply that we can think our way to a spiritual life, but many of us do not come from such a tradition. So what can we do?

If we start our search with the idea, the ideology, the theory, or the theology, we may find ourselves unable to find anything. As Theresa of Avila said, the biggest obstacle to finding God is our assumptions about what we are looking for.

The African American spiritual "Over My Head" offers a key that can help us take advantage of the full freedom that is our spiritual birthright:

> Over my head, I hear music in the air.
> Over my head, I hear music in the air.
> Over my head, I hear music in the air.
> There must be a God somewhere.

It's because we hear the music—because we have had a first-hand, unqualified, unfiltered experience of the sacred and the holy—that we can say with conviction, "There must be a God somewhere." The experience precedes the theology. Rather than trying to fit the experience into a predefined concept, we can define the concepts only in light of what we have learned in our lives. This may seem radical, yet it is the path that mystics and contemplatives have been suggesting from time immemorial.

If you long to connect with the Sacred, if you desire to live a life that is more in touch with the Holy, stop listening for something and start simply listening. If you have given up on an anthropomorphic deity—the old white guy with the long white beard, or any of his stand-ins—yet can't figure out what to put in its place, stop looking for something and start simply looking around you. Notice those places in your life where you have felt yourself in the presence of the Holy, remember those experiences in which you have heard your connectedness; seek in your own life—your own feelings, your own moments—those places where you have encountered, or are encountering, the Sacred. In other words, simply pray. Pray without any preconceived notion of what you're doing or why. Simply do it, and see what happens.

After you pray, *then* begin to think. Think about what your experiences tell you about the holy. Think about what those experiences tell you about the way the world works and the spirit moves. Build your theology on your experience, rather than the other way around. Define the divine for yourself through your own experiences rather than seeking experiences that match someone else's definition.

Moses, for example, was so surprised to encounter his God in a burning bush at Mount Horeb that he had to be told he was standing on holy ground and to take off his shoes. This just wasn't where God was supposed to be, so Moses had a hard time recognizing it. And we, too, often can't see where the sacred is moving in our lives because of what we've been taught to expect. So many people have given up on religion—on God—because they look and look where they've been told to look but always end up feeling disappointed.

And that is why I know of no more important activity than prayer. Connecting and reconnecting to the source of our lives, to that sacred mystery "in which we live, and move, and have our being," as the Apostle Paul puts it, is essential if we are to live full and rich lives. A biblical Psalmist paints a wonderful picture:

> Blessed is the one who . . . meditates day and night. Such a one is like a tree planted by streams of water, which yields its fruit in season and whose leaf does not wither. Whatever she or he does prospers.

A Buddhist teacher puts it like this:

> Studying the truth speculatively is a useful way of collecting preaching material. But remember that unless you meditate constantly your light of truth may go out.

According to these traditions, prayer is not just something to do in times of desperation or gratitude. In order to get the most out of a spiritual practice you must practice it regularly, until it becomes a habit, a constant in your life. Throughout time and across cultures students have asked their teachers, gurus, shamans, and mystics to share the art and technique of connecting and communing with the holy and the sacred through prayer. "Teach us to pray," the Christian Gospels of Matthew and Luke both record the disciples of Jesus asking him. Many sutras within the Buddhist traditions consist of nothing but Siddhartha's explanations of the methods he advocates for spiritual practice. The Hindu *Bhagavad Gita* is, itself, an extended instruction by Shiva of Arjuna in the way of spiritual living.

Each tradition has its own Way, its own method, to offer modern-day seekers. Yet many today find that the answers given in the past do not speak to them. For some, the problem is that these answers seem to have been not only codified but calcified—at some point the once living method became a museum's lesson, no longer an open door but a carved stone tablet. Others find that the answers are so generalized they don't seem to speak to their needs as individuals. Still others see these answers as so steeped in a particular time or tradition that they do not grant access to anyone but the inmost of the in crowd.

All too often this stagnation can result in people becoming "cultural Christians," or Buddhists, or Hindus—only attending to the outward formalities of the faith—even though these traditions encourage individuals, in the contexts of their own communities, to deepen their lives through regular practice of their faith. Unitarian Universalist minister Scott Alexander writes in *Everyday Spiritual Practice* of his tradition: "Every individual is expected, with the help of clergy and community, to nurture and tend the garden of his or her own religious life each and every day."

Many of us today describe ourselves as religious eclectics, open to and interested in learning from a number of religious paths. Perhaps you were raised in a Christian church and at some point rejected the tradition in which you were raised, seeking now in distant religious lands or in the so-called "secular realms" of science and psychology. Or perhaps you stayed in the church you grew up in but have never felt the fit to be quite right—you find yourself challenging and questioning the things you are taught. Maybe you were raised outside of institutionalized religions altogether, yet have an abiding interest in spiritual matters. Perhaps you have a Bible on the bookshelf, but next to it are Richard Bach, Daniel Quinn, Mary Daly, Carlos Castaneda, Joseph Campbell, Joanna Macy, Ram Dass, the Dalai Lama, Caroline Myss, Thich Nhat Hanh, or Starhawk. For many of us, our religious practices are as likely to be an amalgam of traditions as they are to be from any one particular practice.

The thread that often runs through the wanderings of such spiritual seekers is an interest in the mystical—the belief that the Transcendent can be touched, that Ultimate Reality can be directly experienced. Many of us have a deep interest in the myriad of practices that the world's various religious traditions have developed to facilitate (or, perhaps more accurately, to train for) this experience. Unfortunately, our interest is often frustrated because these practices, which have been developed within a specific religious context, frequently feel particular to that context. To use them feels like inappropriate appropriation, and the fit is rarely quite right.

Raised in liberal Presbyterian and Methodist churches (or more precisely, their summer camp programs), I wandered widely in my own quest for a spiritual practice that was deep enough to really help me reach out beyond myself, yet also broad enough for my eclectic tastes and experiences. My "homemade" practices often felt inauthentic, yet the traditionally sanctioned "authentic" practices felt too limited. In divinity school, I made an academic cross-cultural study of monastic practices to see if I could discover—or create—an approach that was at once both innovative and grounded in tradition.

When I looked past the specific practices, I found core elements that are common across the religious landscape. There are four types of prayer practiced in one form or another by every religious tradition. Christianity calls them *praise and thanksgiving, confession, meditation,* and *intercession.* I call them *Naming, Knowing, Listening,* and *Loving. Naming* the many ways that the holy and the sacred move in our lives and in the wider world; *knowing* ourselves fully, in both our strengths and weaknesses; *listening* to that "voice of quiet stillness" that resides in each of us; and reaching out in *loving* concern to the world around us.

Looking at the form of prayer rather than its content—at the *how* of it rather than the *why* or to *whom*—can point the way toward the development of a modern prayer practice that is free of specific metaphors and images, not tied to any particular religious worldview, and not demanding adherence to any one set of religious symbols and expressions. This form of prayer can be the basis for a framework that can support a variety of religious beliefs, without depending on any in particular, creating an inclusive, yet rooted prayer practice.

Even so, you may be asking, *What of the content?* Are we praying to someone when we pray, and if we are, who or what is it? If prayer is asking for something, whom are we asking? If it's about building a relationship, to whom do we relate?

And what if you don't believe in any "sacred something"? Is prayer still worth your while? What merit can there be in an "invented" prayer practice? Weren't all the real prayer practices developed (or revealed) long ago and handed down through generations? How do you know that what you're doing is worth doing if you just made it up?

Within the Jewish, Christian, and Muslim traditions it has been taught that prayer is communication—a conversation—with God. Many neo-Pagans often address a variety of divinities—Father, Mother, Lady, Lord, or a variety of other names—but there is still the image of a "person" with whom to talk. Even though it is held up as an example of a non-theistic religion, there are Buddhist sects in which adherents pray to Amidha Buddha. For some of us, the idea of a personal God presents a serious hurdle in bringing prayer practices into our lives. The exclusive "old white guy with the long white beard" is no longer an accepted or acceptable image—and neither, for many, is the great Earth Mother or any kind of Cosmic Person. Yet the idea of prayer as praying *to* something is so ingrained that it is hard to imagine the one without the other. Simply put, to whom do you pray when your god is a what? How do you have a conversation with an inanimate, or impersonal, force?

This can be a real struggle. It has been for me—not only in my own spiritual life but also in the writing of this book. Do I use traditional "God talk" or stay away from that language completely, knowing the real trouble it causes some people? My own experience is that the practices I describe here, among others, have shown me new ways to reclaim the old language. I found that it was me who was rigid and inflexible, not the words. And by reclaiming this traditional language I have regained access to the beauty, wisdom, and power of these traditions, passed down through the ages.

And these traditions themselves teach that we shouldn't get too caught up in the words and images we use. Christianity, for instance, includes strong admonitions against trying to have too clear an image of the Divine. Anthony Bloom, an archbishop in the Russian Orthodox Christian Church, warns in *Beginning to Pray*, "the moment you try to focus on an imaginary god, or a god you can imagine, you are in great danger of placing an idol between yourself and the real God." This is reminiscent of the famous phrase of the fifth-century Catholic theologian Augustine, who says, "*si comprehendis non es deus*" ("If you comprehend it, it's not God"). The thirteenth-century mystic Theresa of Avila notes that "the greatest obstacle to your experience of God is your last experience of God." The image you bring to the encounter can get in the way of a true encounter, for you see what you expect to see instead of what is actually there.

When Jesus' disciples ask him how they should pray, his answer begins, "Pray *like this . . .*" It is the attitude or perspective that is most important. This qualification implies that his answer was to offer a pattern rather than to set forth a particular set of words. Jesus, like a myriad of other teachers before and since, offers his companions a model, an example to be adopted and adapted rather than slavishly copied. The practice suggested here draws on many of these models and adapts them to the modern mind.

Anthony Bloom writes, "Prayer is an encounter, a relationship which is deep, and this relationship cannot be forced either on us or God." Each type of prayer—whether a request or a declaration of remorse—can be seen as a step in the development and evolution of our relationship with the Holy, just as each time we compliment a friend, share some of our joy, or ask for help, we deepen the friendship. Bloom's words offer reassurance. The quality of our prayer experience, its efficacy, is not entirely up to us. Our prayer occurs in the context of a relationship, so what we do is only part of the equation.

Yet what if you still can't get past *God*, however flexibly and creatively the word is used? Researchers, including Dr. Herbert

Benson, professor at the Harvard Medical School, have demonstrated quite forcefully the positive benefits that accrue to even a "secular" spiritual practice. Each of the four types of prayer has not only religious roots but non-religious manifestations as well. Prayers of Thanksgiving, for instance, are echoed in the therapeutic practice of keeping a gratitude journal, and the religious practice of Confession has a secular counterpart in, among other places, the "fearless moral inventory" of the Twelve Step Movement. Such practices can be well worth the effort even if there is no one and nothing to whom—or to which—they are directed.

Yet if the mystics are correct, if prayer is a conversation with the Sacred Mystery, if it is the means by which a relationship develops between us and the holy, then we can trust that our partner in that relationship will be revealed in and through our conversations. We don't need to know what the Mystery is like before we begin praying. As with any other friendship we have had, we will come to know our friend through the relationship itself.

For now, let us think of prayer.

WE CALL IT PRAYER

When the mind knows, we call it knowledge.

When the heart knows, we call it love.

When the being knows, we call it prayer.

—Osho

Naming

The Pilgrims were not thankful because they survived the winter. They survived the winter because they were thankful.

—Peter Fleck

IN THE BOOK OF EXODUS, Moses encounters the Divine in a burning bush, and the Divine gives him a mission to free the people of Israel from their bondage in Egypt. Not too unreasonably, Moses asks what he should reply when people ask who sent him. "I am that I am," is the reply. "Tell them 'I Am' has sent you." The Hebrew *Eheyeh asher Eheyeh* is quite interesting, because it has no tense. It can be translated as "I am who I am," "I was who I was," "I will be who I will be," or any combination of these. In essence, the reply identifies God as existence itself—pure being unbound by time or place.

While it might seem that the answer given to Moses is pretty complete, the Hebrew Scriptures are full of ways of calling out to *Eheyeh asher Eheyeh*. In Genesis alone, God is called by three different names—Yahweh, Elohim, and Jehovah. In fact, throughout the Hebrew Scriptures there are more than fifty different terms used: Among other things, God is called *El Shaddai* (God Almighty, or Self-Sufficient), *Jehovah-Rophe* (The Lord Who Heals), *Abhir* (Mighty One), *El-Olam* (Everlasting God), *El Roi* (God of Seeing, or, The God Who Opens Our Eyes), and *Eyaluth*

(Strength). At different times, people understood each of these as ways of naming the Divine. Ultimately, however, a prohibition grew up about uttering the name of God, because it was realized that a person could become so attached to a particular name—and the images and ideas of God that would go along with it—that the name would in effect become an idol. (This is why you often will see the word *God* written with the vowel missing—G-d—in Jewish writing.) For this reason, a recent translation of the Torah uses the phrase, "Name that cannot be named."

Some might think that in the Christian tradition there is only one name for God or, at least, only three, taking the names of the Trinity into account. Yet in the New Testament Jesus is called many names: Shepherd of the Sheep, Bishop and Guardian of our Souls, Daystar, Deliverer, Advocate, Last (or Second) Adam, Ancient of Days, Chief Cornerstone, Immanuel, First Born, Head of the Body, Physician, Root of Jesse, Chief Apostle, Great High Priest, Pioneer and Perfecter of our Faith, Christ, Logos, Sophia, and Alpha and Omega. If we look beyond scripture to tradition, Christianity has ascribed many other appellations to the Divine.

In the Islamic tradition, God has ninety-nine names. Some are found in the Qur'an itself and others in the Hadith, the collected sayings of the Prophet Mohammed, yet all are recognized as ways of understanding, and therefore naming, the sacred One. Some examples are *al-Rahman* (The Compassionate), *al-Rahim* (The Merciful), *al-Ghaffar* (The Great Forgiver), *al-Latif* (The Subtle), *al-Wasi'* (The Vast, The All-Embracing), *al-Batin* (The Hidden), *al-Sabur* (The Patient).

Foundational to Islam is the declaration that "there is no God but God," yet still the tradition recognizes that that one God has many names; no one name can convey the totality that is Allah. It is said that there is actually a hundredth name but that it, like the ultimate truth of the One God, is a mystery.

Even a hundred names do not exhaust humanity's understandings of the Divine. Outside of the Abrahamic faiths of Judaism, Christianity, and Islam, the penchant for naming the

Sacred is similarly varied. In *She Who Is*, Elizabeth Johnson notes that a survey of names used within the many indigenous African religions reveals such names as *the Architect of the World, the One who sees all, the One you confide your troubles to, the One who can turn everything upside down, the One there from ancient times, the One who gives to all, the One who bears the world, the One who loves*, and perhaps the most intriguing, *the One who has not let us down yet.*

The Hindu tradition recognizes thousands of divinities—each, of course, with their own names—yet understands them all to be essentially manifestations of one overarching reality. A person might have a particular goddess or god to whom they regularly pray, yet she can use any one of the names depending on her need at any given time. Different people can pray to different gods while still knowing themselves to be praying to the same ultimate reality. One of Hinduism's many gifts is the understanding that differing names don't have to be divisive.

All of this diversity demonstrates, even among traditions that teach a belief in one God, that human beings have spent a great deal of time and energy trying to name the sacred, and for a variety of reasons. First, naming and categorizing things seems to be a significant human drive. In the book of Genesis, for example, there is a story told of all the animals parading past Adam, the first human, so that he might name them. Ancients believed that knowing something's name meant knowing its essence and having power over it. The compulsion to name things may simply reflect our desire to understand. Humans process experience with language and so we need language to make sense of things. Recognizing that there is no language that can fully comprehend the totality of the Divine, the Christian theologian Augustine argued that we must therefore give God many names so as to avoid the difficulty of coming to think that the name we use captures the essence of the God we seek. And so we have.

When we know someone well, we know him or her by name. Knowing a name is the first step to building a relationship. That's why there are so many cultural protocols for handling introductions. Sharing names is the beginning of real connection, and religions have always, despite their outward seeming differences, been about helping people to make connections with the depth of life—their own lives and the wider life of which we are all a part.

Naming that "wider life," then, is a first step in establishing a relationship with it, and therefore, Naming prayer is one of the most fundamental types of prayer in all religious traditions. It provides us with a chance to name the Sacred—to give voice to how and where we have encountered the Holy or where we have felt the Divine in our lives.

There are Baha'i prayers that consist of virtually nothing but lists of names and attributes of the Divine. The Long Healing Prayer begins, "God is the Healer, the Sufficer, the Helper, the All-Forgiving, the All-Merciful. I call on Thee O Exalted One, O Faithful One, O Glorious One! Thou the Sufficing, Thou the Healing, Thou the Abiding, O Thou Abiding One . . . ." The prayer goes on in that way for several pages with many names you would expect as well as some surprises. Often the list contains startling juxtapositions such as, "O Thou Known to all, O Thou Hidden from all," and "O Most Manifest . . . O Concealed One." Such a prayer might be called a meditation on the qualities and character of God. This is certainly one way Muslims understand meditation on the ninety-nine names of Allah.

It has been said that we cannot see what we don't look at, and Naming prayer encourages us to look at our lives to see where and how the sacred is present. Perhaps, in your life right now, you are experiencing the divine as "Comforter." Or, perhaps, for you right now, it is "the One who churns things up." Naming prayer calls on you to engage the ancient Adamic practice of giving a name to what you see.

If, as the world's mystics suggest, the Mystery is fundamentally relational, naming is necessary for relationship. We need to name to know, and since the purpose of prayer—or one of the purposes, at least—is to get to know ourselves and life itself at the deepest levels, this practice of naming provides a foundation upon which a relationship may be built.

On the other hand, there are many people in the world today who do not believe in any kind of "personal God," and for whom talk of "relationship" seems outdated and unnecessarily romantic. Naming prayer does not require a Sacred Other; instead, it can allow an opportunity to lift up all for which you are thankful at this moment, all the blessings and miracles in your life, all the joy in your living. Take your time. "Count your blessings," as the old phrase says. Don't feel embarrassed by the riches in your life. Don't worry about becoming prideful—gratitude is one of the great antidotes to pride. The thirteenth-century Christian mystic Miester Eckhart writes, "If in your lifetime you can pray only one prayer and it is 'Thank You,' it will be sufficient." Cultivating gratitude is fundamental to the vast majority of the world's religious traditions as well as to an individual's spiritual growth.

In a famous experiment, participants were divided into three groups: Testers asked one group to spend five minutes at the end of each day writing in a journal all the things that had happened that day for which they were thankful, a second group was asked to spend five minutes writing all that had gone wrong, and a control group did neither. As you might guess, those who spent time focusing on the good in their lives reported at the end of the experiment that their general sense of well-being had improved and that they saw the world as a pretty good place, while those who focused on the negative reported just the opposite. Spending some time each day in Naming prayer—naming and noting the ways in which the sacred is moving in your life and reminding yourself of all you have to be thankful for—might just tip the balance toward seeing the glass as (at least) half full.

Whether you are reflecting on the attributes of the holy or stopping to notice where and how the holy has touched your own life, Naming prayer can provide a grounding for every other kind of prayer.

Knowing

Lord, we ain't what we ought to be
And we ain't what we want to be
And we ain't what we gonna be, but Thank God
we ain't what we were.

—Traditional prayer

"THOU HAS SEARCHED ME and known me, O my God," sings the Psalmist, yet it is at least equally important, and perhaps more so, to know yourself. "*Gnothi seauton*" was the admonition inscribed over the portal to the Greek Oracle of Delphi—"Know thyself." It might seem that of all people we know ourselves best, yet we are in fact most often more mystified by ourselves than by anyone else. With prayers of *Knowing*—in the Christian tradition often called prayers of confession—we have an opportunity to fully reflect on our life as it is today, and especially to recognize those places that call for reconciliation and atonement.

We are all a mixture of saint and sinner, and this stop on our journey is an opportunity to see and know ourselves in all our subtle shadings. This is not a call for guilt or self-criticism but for honest self-appraisal. Unless we acknowledge our faults and failings, we can do nothing about overcoming them. This type of prayer allows us the opportunity to give voice to the broken, wounded, worried places in our souls. It is the chance to take a "fearless moral inventory," to use the language of the Twelve Step Movement, and to give voice to what lurks in the shadows. The life of the spirit calls on us to be authentic, whole people, and knowing where we are weak and wounded is essential to meeting this challenge.

There is no question that most of us would rather not look at certain aspects of ourselves. It's been said that most people think that there are only three perfect people in this world . . . and that they look forward to meeting the other two! Yet that's only a surface assessment. Most people, if they are honest, would more likely empathize with the novice Buddhist monk who confesses, "I believe that all things have Buddha-nature . . . except me." Most of us have an inner judge who declares us unworthy, who tells us we're not good enough—strong enough, smart enough, whatever enough.

This may be, at least in part, because we've inherited or adopted impossible role models. "Be thou perfect, as your Heavenly Father is perfect," Jesus is remembered as saying, and many people try to live up to some version of this injunction. *Be a man like John Wayne or Clint Eastwood. Be a real woman—with a career, a family, and a fulfilling personal life. Be as successful as your older brother, or as creative as your younger sister. You can never be too rich or too thin. Be thou perfect.* It's no wonder that, even if only when they wake in the middle of the night, most people fear that they don't measure up.

In Al-Anon there is a saying: "Progress, not perfection." In other words, we shouldn't focus on attaining some imagined and longed-for state of perfection. Rather than hold ourselves to such an impossible standard, we should look to the process we're involved in and the progress we're making each and every day as the measure of our lives. In keeping with taking things one day at a time, this saying reminds us that none of us is perfect—that we all have things to learn, areas in which we can grow—and that we ought not to assess ourselves by what we are not but by what we are. Still, it might be possible to reclaim the word *perfection*. In fact, it might be possible to recast the Al-Anon slogan as, "Progress *is* perfection."

The Vietnamese poet and Buddhist monk Thich Nhat Hanh writes about the perfection of trees. Trees are perfect because they are just trees; they don't try to be anything else. They do nothing but "tree things." Trees simply *are* and, thus, are perfect. One of the primary insights of Shakyamuni Buddha, usually recorded as his first words upon gaining enlightenment, is that, "Everything is perfect *just as it is.*" Trees are perfect trees, stars are perfect stars, and we are perfect, fallible human beings.

This may seem like a contradiction, perhaps an oxymoron— "perfectly imperfect"—yet it makes a lot of sense if we can free ourselves from the notion that perfection implies some kind of permanent state that is achieved and then maintained. What in the world is permanent like that? The perfect blue sky is always in fluid motion; the perfect field of daffodils is always changing. If you were to freeze the perfect lake—to prevent all change and movement within it—you would soon have nothing more than a stagnant puddle, a breeding ground for mosquitoes. Life is change, growth, movement. Perfection, then, is not about becoming something that we're not, but fully being what we are.

Ironically, this is the core of the Christian teachings on sin and grace, teachings that have often been terribly misconstrued and which, when mistakenly understood, are at the root of many people's feelings of failure. "We are all sinners," was never meant as a condemnation, but rather a simple description, like "We are all air breathers." If all of us are sinners then none of us is supposed to be anything else—it's fundamental to who we all are. "All have fallen short of the glory of God" is not a judgment but an observation, like "Everybody's forgetful from time to time," or "All of us occasionally lose our tempers." Rather than an indictment of how far we are from the ideal, the heart of the theology of sin is a message of freedom: We don't have to work so hard at trying to be—or, at least, appearing to be—"perfect" because, let's face it, none of us is and none of us ever will be.

That's why teachings on sin are always supposed to be coupled with teachings on grace. "We are all sinners . . ." is meant to be coupled to the equally important truth, "God loves us anyway." That's the good news that is so often missed, yet it can be found in various forms in all of the world's major religions. When Hindus and Wiccans greet the God and Goddess in the people they meet, when Buddhists see Buddha-nature as pervading all things, they are merely offering variations of the teaching "Everything is perfect just as it is." "Just as it is," of course, meaning as it really is—flaws and all.

Yet if all of that is true, why should we spend time in this confessional Knowing prayer? If it's not about feeling guilty for our failures, what is it about? Won't it bring us back to focusing on what we're not rather than on what we are? Won't it just serve to make us feel badly about ourselves?

Not necessarily. There's a Christian saying that can prove helpful: "God loves you just the way you are, and loves you too much to let you stay that way." Acknowledging that our flaws and weaknesses are common to the whole human community does not make them any less flaws and weaknesses. Recognizing that it is human not only to err but to out-and-out fail does not suddenly make successes of our failures. Broken and wounded places in our souls and psyches are still broken and wounded, even though we don't need to feel guilty about them. In other words, the idea that "Progress is perfection" still implies the need for progress.

It is, then, vitally important to become aware of the places where we need to shore ourselves up. We can't resolve not to do something if we haven't first recognized that it doesn't serve us or the world we live in; we can't improve something that we don't notice needs improvement. It is crucial to take the time to really look at all the ways we have let down our own best selves, all the ways we have failed to live up to what we know we are capable of, if we're going to make any progress toward that better self. This need not be cause for self-condemnation; rather, it can bring together the relief of acceptance and the gentle encouragement toward improvement.

At another level, this Knowing prayer is essential because we won't be able to believe that we are "perfect, flaws and all," if we're unwilling to look at those flaws. As long as we relegate parts of ourselves to the dark corners of our spirit we continue to reinforce the notion that there are parts of us that are unacceptable because we, ourselves, are unable to accept them. Praying about the broken and fragile places in our lives is not about seeking God's understanding and forgiveness—which the theology of grace in all of its forms assures us we already have—but about seeking our own. Can *we* embrace our whole selves? Can we acknowledge the dual nature of our existence and still declare it all good? We can only rest in life's embrace or truly embrace others if our answer is "yes."

Knowing prayer encourages us to look unblinkingly at the wounded and broken places in ourselves, seeing the ways these wounds continue to hobble us and may continue wounding others. From the petty to the seriously problematic, we look at all of the parts of ourselves that we'd rather not see so that we can come to terms with the fact—and it is a fact—that these are part of who we are. Acknowledging this doesn't make us any less. It actually makes us more—more whole, more complete, more authentic. The life of prayer is a life moving toward greater and greater authenticity.

Knowing prayer is not a mere recitation of things we've been told we're not supposed to do. We may begin by examining specific acts, but the deeper we go in this prayer the more we begin to explore the attitudes that are at the base of those acts and may even be infused in some of the supposedly "good" things we've done. A generous act done with selfish motivations can be, from this perspective, no different than an act of explicit selfishness. In the Sermon on the Mount, Jesus called us to value ethics over actions, and to examine the inner movements of heart and mind that spark those acts. This same teaching can be found in all of the world's religions. How and why we do what we do is at least as important as the things we do, and Knowing prayer helps us to assess these inner, and often unseen, dimensions of ourselves.

Carl Jung thought it absolutely essential for people to come to grips with what he called "the shadow." He writes, "To mix a metaphor, the shadow is a tight pass, a narrow door, whose painful constriction is spared to no one who climbs down into the deep wellspring. But one must learn to know oneself in order to know who one is." The good news, though, is that on the other side of this "narrow door" is a boundless expanse. After one confronts the less-than parts of oneself—which invariably makes a person feel small—there is an even greater opening up that reveals a reality far beyond anything previously imagined. Jung describes it as a place with "apparently no inside and no outside, no above and no below, no here and no there, no mine and no thine, no good and no bad . . . . where I am inseparably this and that, and this and that are I."

This time of Knowing prayer, then, is not so much an obligation as an opportunity to more fully and truly accept ourselves *because* we are willing to prayerfully look at our brokenness and failings. It's an opportunity to find release from the stranglehold of our secrets, to free ourselves from the fear of exposure, because we realize we have nothing to hide. *All* of us have fallen short of the glory of God. We don't have to descend into the hell of self-recrimination, we can experience the heaven of true self-acceptance.

Perhaps the American physicist Alfred Romer puts it best when he writes, "There has come to me an insight into the meaning of Darkness. The reason one must face his [or her] darkness, and enter into that darkness, is not that he [or she] may return purified to face God. One must go into the darkness because that is where God is." Knowing prayer is an invitation to take that journey.

Listening

There is guidance for each of us, and by lowly listening, we shall hear the right word. Certainly there is a right for you that needs no choice on your part. Place yourself in the middle of the stream of power and wisdom which flows into your life. Then, without effort, you are impelled to truth and to perfect contentment.

—Ralph Waldo Emerson

LANGUAGE ITSELF IS ONE of the greatest challenges in a cross-cultural study of prayer practices. In Western traditions, *contemplative prayer* is the silent, effortless emptying of one's self so that you can become aware of yourself as filled with what the Catholic contemplative Father Thomas Keating calls "the Ultimate Mystery, beyond thoughts, words, and emotions." In these traditions, *meditation,* on the other hand, is the concentrated mulling and musing on a specific topic; meditating on a passage of scripture, for instance, means thinking deeply about it. So *contemplation* and *meditation,* which many think of as synonyms, are actually antonyms.

Both of these kinds of practice can be found in Eastern traditions as well, of course, but the terminology is exactly reversed. In Buddhism, for example, *meditation* is the emptying of self and *contemplation* is the term for focused concentration. When comparing the literature, then, you need to know whether you're comparing the same terms or the same practices.

One way around this confusion is to use the Greek terms *apophatic* and *kataphatic*, terms that are used to describe both theological perspectives and spiritual practices. A kataphatic theological stance says that the sacred can be apprehended through words and images, and the corresponding practices make use of both. Apophatic theology, on the other hand, asserts that the divine cannot be apprehended through words and images and so its practices are wordless and imageless.

For our purposes, Listening prayer corresponds with the apophatic approach—the West's contemplation and the East's meditation. It is a silencing prayer, a centering prayer, a prayer that quietly frees us from the clutter and cacophony that generally reign over our interior worlds. This type of prayer is not about words and ideas but about gently and easily moving from all forms of doing to a simple state of being.

At the same time, we live in a word-oriented culture. We are bombarded with words on a daily basis. It has been said that language is one of the few things that differentiates us from the rest of the animal kingdom. Language is the lens through which we perceive the world or, at least, by which we are able to understand it. The idea of experience without words is, for many, inconceivable. Yet it is possible. The author Madeleine L'Engle writes, "I, who live by words, am wordless when I try my words in prayer. All language turns to silence. Prayer will take my words and then reveal their emptiness."

Such a space of silence is not only possible, say the mystics and contemplatives, it is absolutely essential. In the Hebrew Psalms, God says, "Be still and know that I am God." This encouragement can be heard in every one of the world's major religions. Be still and listen to the divine spark, the Buddha-nature, the movement of the Tao that is inherent in us all. Listening prayer is predicated on the notion that God is already speaking to us and that the reason we don't know this is that our heads are so full of static.

Think about it for a moment. Stop right now and note the number of thoughts and impressions that are swirling around your head as you read this chapter. Some may have something to do with the words you are reading, but most probably do not. Instead, you are most likely ticking off shopping lists, replaying a fight you had with someone at work, remembering something the kids said, or thinking about something you need to be doing. If so much is going on in your mind when you're quietly engaged in reading a book, how much more is happening when you're actively engaged in doing things in the world?

Buddhists often use the term *monkey mind* to describe the way our minds leap from subject to subject frenetically. Like a monkey swinging from branch to branch, hopping and hooting, never staying still for long, there is a fairly constant chatter in our minds, and this chatter is not conducive to prayer. Mystic and contemplative traditions insist that a certain amount of stillness—both inner and outer—is absolutely necessary for the deepest and most "effective" prayer. There are many reasons for this.

Consider the biblical story of Elijah hiding in the mouth of a cave as God passes by. The New International Version translates it this way:

> . . . a great and powerful wind tore the mountains apart and shattered the rocks before the Lord, but the Lord was not in the wind. After the wind there was an earthquake, but the Lord was not in the earthquake. After the earthquake came a fire, but the Lord was not in the fire. And after the fire came a gentle whisper. When Elijah heard it, he pulled his cloak over his face and went out and stood at the mouth of the cave.

One translation of this passage renders the phrase "gentle whisper" as "a voice of quiet stillness," and the most common translation is "a still, small voice," but the import is the same in all versions. God does not speak in thunderous tones that can drown out the drone of our inner monologues. The call of the sacred is quiet, so that in even the stillest of rooms we'd have to strain to hear it. This is the importance of Listening prayer.

Another premise upon which Listening prayer is based is the immanence of God. The sacred is not something "out there," far removed from us, requiring a shout to be heard. Rather, as the Bible has it, God is "closer than our own breathing," or as the Qur'an puts it, "closer than the throbbing vein in our necks." The Shalem Institute for Spiritual Formation teaches that the essence of prayer is learning how to quiet ourselves to the point that we can hear the prayer God is already praying within us. Thomas Keating, one of the monks who developed the Catholic prayer practice known as Centering Prayer, writes that God is, "closer than breathing, closer than thinking, closer than choosing—closer than consciousness itself."

Yet how often do we miss precisely that which is closest to us? In our hectic and harried lives it is the thing right under our own noses that seems to go unnoticed most often. The poet T. S. Eliot asks, "Where is the Life we have lost in living?" which is reminiscent of a well-known passage from *Walden* in which Henry David Thoreau asks,

> Why should we live in such a hurry and waste of life? . . . I wish to live deliberately . . . I wish to learn what life has to teach, and not, when I come to die, discover that I have not lived . . . . I do not wish to live what is not life . . . .

In one way or another all of the great spiritual teachers have critiqued the kind of life that is "not life"—life that is lived at high speed, jamming something into every moment, never pausing just to be. "We are not human doings, we are human beings," the bumper sticker says, yet one would be hard pressed to prove it by looking in most people's datebooks. People today are often so overly programmed that it would take a powerful wind, an earthquake, *and* a fire to catch our attention—yet the wisdom of that ancient Jewish story is that the sacred whispers rather than shouts. Listening prayer helps us to turn down the volume of our lives.

This chapter began by noting that language itself is a major hurdle to talking about contemplative prayer. It also presents a challenge to engaging in such prayer. Language tends to distance us from and limit our experiences of life. When we have an experience and put words to it—loneliness for example—we immediately burden it with every other experience of loneliness we've ever known. No longer does this experience stand alone, unique; it becomes unavoidably colored by past associations and other expectations of it.

Ralph Waldo Emerson writes, "These roses under my window make no reference to former roses or to better ones; they are for what they are; they exist with God today." Far too often, however, every rose we see exists for us only in relation to "former" or "better" ones. And not just roses, of course. Every new thing we encounter is assessed by how closely it resembles, and in what ways it differs from, other things we've seen. Even old and familiar things are viewed through lenses made up of every piece of history we have with them.

This is true of our relationships, as well. How often do we really see a person as he or she is right at that moment? "You've always been a screw up," we say, or, "You're just like your mother was." Just as we compare new things, we compare new people to our mental inventory—"You remind me of my cousin Ned," or, "I've never known a minister like you before!" If we're totally honest with ourselves, not even we are seen "for what we are" but are forever compared against "former" or "better" versions of ourselves.

The Christian saint Theresa of Avila once said, "The greatest obstacle to your experience of God is your last experience of God." Tom Driver, in his seminal book *Christ in a Changing World* writes, "The Christ of faith is not the one we knew yesterday but the one we expect to meet while going forward." If life is change and growth and movement, then certainly this is true of the sacred, no matter how many theologians have argued for God's immutability. To truly have a relationship with the sacred, then, we have to find some way to free ourselves from all the words and images we attach to it and that threaten to enshrine it in our previous experiences of it so that we can meet it as it is today. Listening prayer is one way to do this.

There are many techniques for Listening prayer. In the Zen Buddhist tradition, you would usually begin by counting your breaths—in-breaths and out-breaths—one number on each breath until you've reached ten, and then begin again. In the Catholic tradition of Centering Prayer, you choose a single word—a name or attribute of God, perhaps—and repeat it gently whenever you notice yourself thinking; otherwise simply sit in silence.

That's the essence of apophatic practice. As the title of a recent best seller by Sylvia Boorstein puts it, *Don't Just Do Something, Sit There!* Since the essence of these practices is on being still rather than doing something to make one's self still, the ideal form would be to simply sit in stillness, body and mind. Yet this is incredibly difficult to do because of the impatient restlessness of monkey mind, or, to use another Zen metaphor, because of the voraciousness of the hungry tiger that is our mind. In their wisdom, contemplative traditions often recommend giving the tiger a certain amount of "meat" to keep it quiet. That's where the sacred word, or the repeated mantra, or the counting of breaths comes from. Each of these things gives the mind a little something to do while it learns to do nothing.

Essentially all apophatic practices train us to become observers rather than commentators. Have you ever sat by a river and suddenly become aware that you've been watching it but have not been thinking anything about it? Or for that matter, about much of anything else? That experience is the goal of Listening prayer.

At first, you will notice a tidal wave of thoughts and feelings, memories and dreams flooding at you. This is where the practice begins—learning to see these thoughts flowing at you without feeling the need to comment on them. For most beginners a practice session will look something like this:

First, you settle down, take a deep breath, and a feeling of peace comes over you. You're counting your breaths—"one, two, three . . ."—and suddenly you realize that you're thinking about what you need to get from the store for dinner. "Shoot," you say, "I got distracted." Then you realize that that realization was another distraction. "I'm never going to get this," you declare, recognizing that that commentary is itself yet another step away from the silent stillness you crave. Eventually you begin to chide yourself. "Stop it," you say. "I won't think another thought." "Oh heck, that was a thought too." "So was that." "Stop it." It continues like this until the practice period is over, or until you give up in frustration and with a feeling of failure.

Buddhists say that quieting the mind is like trying to stop the ripples in a pond. The approach described above, the approach most beginners take—trying to think the mind quiet—is like trying to stop the ripples by hitting them with your hands. Rather than flattening out the ripples, of course, each hand strike only creates more ripples, requiring more frantic patting until soon you're aggressively splashing the water in an attempt to calm the little ripples. This approach is doomed to failure, yet it is what most beginning practitioners do.

Instead, try to not try anything. When you notice that you've been distracted, simply notice the fact and then return to your practice. No commentary. No condemnation. Please recognize that the instruction "simply notice the fact" does not in any way imply that it is easy, or "simple," to do this. Rather, it indicates that the way of doing this, the manner in which it is to be done, is simply. Don't make a big deal out of noticing your distraction; let it be easy, light.

Here's an exercise that might be helpful: Set aside three minutes during which you will look around you without letting your gaze rest long on any one thing. Move steadily from object to object and simply note what you see: "That is a book. That is my arm. That is the floor. That is an M. C. Escher print. That is my partner. That is my son putting a sandwich into the VCR." Try to maintain equanimity, giving no object greater or lesser impor tance, simply noting each thing as it comes into your field of vision and then moving on.

Similarly, in Listening prayer, you simply notice the thoughts and feelings that come into your field of consciousness, striving to maintain equanimity as in the exercise. Some thoughts will be obviously trivial and others will carry a lot of emotional weight; try to treat them all as exactly the same. Notice them, and then move on.

One of the challenges many people face is determing how to respond to what we might call productive thoughts. A writer who has been trying to find the ending to a short story suddenly sees it perfect and whole while in the midst of Listening prayer. The solution to a problem at work, or in a relationship, bursts forth fully-formed as Athena from the head of Zeus. It makes sense to let all other kinds of thoughts float by, but you know that if you don't jump up and try to capture this insight it will, like a dream, dissolve into mist.

Resist the temptation. If the thought really is important you will remember—eventually—but in the meantime you have set aside this time for this purpose and it will be irretrievably lost if you aren't careful. The only way to create this space is to create it and keep it whole. Silence is broken by the slightest sound, and we have sound enough in our lives. Silence is a precious commodity, and this time of Listening prayer may be one of the only oasis of true, deep silence in the rest of your day. If this prayer really is an opportunity to listen to the divine speaking to you, wouldn't it be rude to get up and take a call while God is talking simply because your cell phone or pager rings?

It is worth noting here the ancient Jewish understanding that a temple should be built not on the most expendable land but on the most fertile soil with the best view. This essentially empty space in which no "productive" thing would be done was given such a prime location because the Jews understood the importance of empty non-productivity, understood the need to be still. This is something that our bottom-line culture has forgotten. Listening prayer is a way of remembering.

What you do with your body is as important as what you do with your mind during Listening prayer—that is, it is both vitally important and doesn't matter all that much. Long before our modern recognition of the body–mind connection, contemplative practitioners in all traditions noted that if you could truly still the body you would still the mind, and vice versa. The cross-legged position of Zen meditation, then, is not in and of itself important except that it is a fairly natural position that can promote a still body.

For many westerners, then, cross-legged would be absolutely the wrong position because the body would continuously call attention to itself. Sitting on a straight-backed chair with feet planted firmly on the floor would make more sense. The position you choose doesn't matter as much as the intent, and perhaps more importantly the effect, of the position: Does it allow you to stay in one place, comfortably, without making you so comfortable that you might get drowsy, and minimize itches and twitches? If so, it is an appropriate posture for apophatic practice. If not, no matter how many monks or masters you've seen doing it, it's not for you.

Perhaps because it does not make use of words or images, Listening prayer is the easiest to see as a structure to which you can bring your own understandings. An Episcopal priest once attended a Zen Buddhist meditation retreat. In one of his interviews with the monastery's abbot, the priest mentioned some apparently mystical experiences he kept having. The abbot advised him to keep at his meditation, noting but paying no particular attention to the experiences, and said that eventually the experiences, the priest, the cushion on which he sat, and the monastery would all dissolve into the Great Nothingness. The priest replied that in his tradition that could never happen because God would always be left. "Same difference," the abbot replied.

Whether one believes that there is an all-encompassing Presence that underlies all that is or that there is an all-encompassing Nothingness underlying all things, the apophatic practice of Listening prayer—in all of its various forms—is aimed to get you past your thoughts of the Ultimate to a direct experience of it.

Loving

> He prayed as he breathed, forming no words and making no
> specific requests, only holding in his heart, like broken birds
> in cupped hands, all those people who were in stress or grief.
>
> —Ellis Peters

PRAYER PRACTICE THAT FOCUSES only on the self is ultimately
hollow, as is a life that is too self-centered. At some point, the
quest for personal peace enlarges into a concern for peace in the
world; the search for self satisfaction broadens to include a desire
that the needs of others be satisfied. We are communal beings by
nature—we live in community and, it can be argued, it is through
community that we are really alive. Rabbis Joseph and Nathan
Segal express it simply: "From you I receive, to you I give; together we share, and by this we live."

The story is told of a monk who was well known in his
monastery for going to the hermitage house for a time of solitary
prayer and meditation. Sometimes he was gone for a week; sometimes it would be a month or more before he returned. One day
he approached the abbot for permission to leave, as he had so
many times before. To everyone's surprise, however, the monk
returned that same afternoon. The abbot asked what had happened to cut short the monk's meditation.

"Nothing," the monk replied. "I have finished my prayers."

The abbot asked why it was so short this time, and the monk replied, "As is my custom, when I arrived at the hermitage I opened the Bible to find a passage on which to meditate. I opened to John 13, which begins with the story of Jesus washing the feet of his disciples at the last supper. I knelt in prayer, yet found myself troubled by the question, 'whose feet can a hermit wash?' I realized that I needed to return to the community."

It is said that the Buddha, at the moment of his enlightenment, seriously considered remaining in the Nirvana he had discovered, yet ultimately decided to return to the world to share what he had learned. As a Zen priest put it, "The mountaintop is enticing, but we must ultimately return to the marketplace." Joseph Campbell points out that this is, in fact, the challenge faced by every hero: Ulysses is tempted to stay on the Sirens' island, Arthur's knights nearly give up their quest for the Holy Grail, and even Dorothy seems to think about staying in Oz. Always, though, the journey must continue to its final destination, a return to the world.

This should not be surprising. Modern psychology has begun to theorize that we are essentially communal beings. While much is made of the importance of *individuation*—the development of our own unique, individual identities—these theorists suggest that it is possible for us to do this only in and through our interactions with others. In a certain sense, we do not exist without these interactions, for these interactions tell us who we are.

The Japanese language provides an illustration. In Japanese there is no equivalent to the English word *I*. In fact, there is not one but six first-person singular pronouns, reflecting the understanding that there is no single, unchanging, and wholly independent self. Who "I" am changes in different social settings. The "I" who is hanging out with a close friend is not exactly the same "I" who is meeting with a respected elder, and neither of these is absolutely identical with the "I" who is meeting someone for the first time. Japanese provides a different word for each of these different "I"s. Western assumptions may make it difficult to grasp this, yet our own experience points to the truth of it. We may believe in an eternal, unchanging self, but we also cherish those people and situations in which we can "be ourselves" because there are so many people and situations in which we can't. It turns out that this may be more than just an expression. It may be that our selves are formed in and through our interactions with others and that, in a certain sense at least, who we are depends on with whom we are with.

Beyond this, there is another truth: We are linked to one another as members of one human family. John Donne writes in *Meditation XVII*, "No man is an island, entire of itself; every man is a piece of the continent, a part of the main; if a clod be washed away by the sea, Europe is the less . . . any man's death diminishes me, because I am involved in mankind . . . ." Martin Luther King Jr. says it more simply in his 1963 "Letter from Birmingham Jail." He writes, "All life is interrelated. We are caught in an inescapable network of mutuality, tied in a single garment of destiny."

What happens to you must, at some level, matter to me, and the deeper you go in the spiritual life, the stronger and clearer this connection becomes. The more one goes into one's self the more obvious it becomes that we are not isolated and alienated individuals—no matter how much it might seem that we are. Hindus, Buddhists, Wiccans, Jews, Christians, Muslims, and seekers on other mystical paths eventually come to see that the Other is the self, that you and I are one.

And so all prayer eventually leads to what we're calling *Loving prayer*. The Christian tradition calls this *petition* or *intercession*, and most people understand this kind of prayer as asking God for something for one's self or for others.

The question often arises why people have to pray to God since God knows all things and should already know the needs of everyone. Many answers have been given, yet one simple one is that we do not pray so that God knows about people's needs; we pray to make sure we know. We engage in Loving prayer to make sure that we are aware of the needs around us, because we most

certainly can do nothing to help a situation—local or global—
that we don't know exists. Whether or not you believe that there
is a "God" listening to your prayers, bringing the needs of others
into your consciousness has merit.

It is so easy to get caught up in the day-to-day details of our
own lives and lose sight of the lives around us, especially if the
lives around us contain pain and suffering. Most of us try our best
to avoid looking at our own wounds, yet we've already seen how
important it is for us to do so if we are to pursue the spiritual
path. It is equally important for us to learn to look on the suffering of others. In the Buddhist Tiep Hien Order, founded by Thich
Nhat Hanh, the fourth precept is:

> Do not avoid contact with suffering or close your eyes
> before suffering. Do not lose awareness of the existence of
> suffering in the life of the world. Find ways to be with those
> who are suffering by all means . . . . awaken yourself and oth-
> ers to the reality of suffering in the world.

It is not easy to look at the world's pain; we want to look away.
It can be overwhelming and nearly paralyzing to consider the
enormity of the problems our planet is facing today. War, famine,
economic and political oppression, environmental degradation—
the list goes on and on. In the face of such seemingly overwhelming challenges, many of us prefer to avert our eyes for fear of
being crushed beneath the weight of our global burdens.

In some ways, it can be even more difficult to see the pain of
the person next to us—to really see it and let it into not just our
minds but into our hearts as well. A common saying is that the
death of thousands is a statistic; the death of one person is a
tragedy. This reflects the psychological truth that it is easier to
empathize with an individual and so, conversely, it is harder to
allow ourselves to truly face the suffering of one person.

That is exactly what we are called to do by Loving prayer.
Loving prayer invites us to open our eyes and our ears, to open
our hearts to the suffering and struggles of people both near to

and far from us, from the details of our neighbor's needs to the dimensions of our world's demands.

As with all prayer, there are ways of simply doing this kind of prayer practice and ways of truly engaging it. Often we are told to draw up lists of people or to accept those offered by our churches and to "pray for the people on the list." This can lead to a rote rendition of "Please God, help Susie who is sick; and Bob who needs a job; and . . ." It can become easy to disengage from the meaning of the words. At the same time, there are a lot of needs in this world, and many of us are stopped before we begin by the idea of a list that would take us a year and a half to get through even once.

Still, the prayer list is one way of attending to Loving prayer. It is not, in and of itself, a bad method. It is important, however, not to merely read your list as you would a shopping list, noting the names but not being affected too deeply. Let the person truly come into your consciousness. To the extent you know of their need, try to make it real to you. Visualize each individual on your list as fully and clearly as you can.

Some people begin with calling each member of their family to mind, striving to make the image of each one a living presence. After that, perhaps, come friends or colleagues, followed by more tangential acquaintances. At last come more national or even global concerns, again trying to make each one more than just a name on a piece of paper. Can you imagine what it would be like if you spent fifteen to thirty minutes each day bringing to mind—in an attitude of loving concern—each of the people who occupy your life and all of the areas in the world that call for your attention?

Note the phrase "call for your attention." A quick scan of the daily newspaper will reveal literally thousands of places and people in the world who are deserving candidates for your Loving prayer. Several dozen countries are right now either engaged in or recovering from some kind of warfare. Millions of people are starving. You cannot pray for them all. This is not a failure on your part; it's a fact. No one person can pray for all of the world's needs—and be truly in touch with and mindful of what she or he is praying about. No one can, but the good news is that no one has to. If you were the only person praying that might be different, but millions of people pray daily. At Unity Village, for instance, the headquarters and home of the Unity School for Christianity, there have been people praying in rotating shifts twenty-four hours a day every day of the year for over one hundred years. And that's just one prayer ministry! You can rest assured that the concerns you don't have on your Loving prayer list are being lifted up by others. Simply put on your list those issues that, for whatever reason, speak to your heart.

Some people don't like the idea of generating a list for prayer. Another approach is to gently allow the "list" to come to you during your prayer rather than begin with a set agenda. This method draws on the idea we've come back to again and again, that our job is to quiet ourselves to the point where we can hear God praying in us. Allow yourself to quiet the chatter of your mind, and see who comes into your consciousness. Assume that this is the person for whom you are to pray. Ask yourself, "What is the prayer I should pray for this person?" and see what comes to mind.

This approach gives theists another answer to the question of why we need to pray to God if God already knows all of our needs. In this case, you move yourself out of the way so that God can tell you who is in need of your prayer. It is not you bringing the petition to God, but the other way around—God is bringing the prayer requests to you.

Of course, you can still profit from this practice even if you don't believe in a personal God who's busy "bringing" things to people and "wanting" you to pray for this or that. Think of it as allowing your subconscious—the psychological equivalent of the "still small voice within"—to bring to your attention that about which you care most. With so much competing for our attention, allowing our inner wisdom to sift through the chaff to find the wheat seems like a worthwhile endeavor. Even if that's all this type of prayer is, it's worth doing. If it's more than that, we'll discover more depth along the way.

An expansion of this practice is to create the space for three people to bubble up in your mind: one with whom you are close, one who is tangential to your life, and one with whom you have need of resolution. In this case you do the same thing three times: Quiet your mind, repeat your intention to pray for someone in one of those three categories, and wait until someone comes to mind. When you finish with one category, move on to the next.

The last category—those with whom we are in need of resolution—may need some explanation. All of us have people in our lives who rub us the wrong way, people whose very presence can annoy and irritate us. There may be people whom we experience this way chronically, and others who have moved into this category because of transient circumstances. There are people we just don't like—never have and probably never will—as well as friends and family members with whom we're currently "on the outs." These are the people we pray for in this third category.

This prayer matters because it does us little good to hold on to negative feelings. Aggravation does all sorts of bad things to our bodies and our minds, not to mention our spirits. It behooves us to try to live by the admonition in the poem "Desiderata": As far as possible without surrender be on good terms with all persons. Taking the time to lovingly pray for the people who grate on our nerves may not do much of anything for them—although it might—but it will almost certainly do a great deal for our own peace of mind.

This brings us to the question of just what happens when we pray for someone. Can prayer heal? Can prayer bring about changes in social conditions? Can we expect to "get what we pray for?"

Mystics have always maintained that we can. Stories of miraculous healings of body, mind, and spirit abound in every religious tradition. Modern Western science is beginning to agree, at least tentatively. Researchers have found, for instance, that the act of praying has a positive effect on the one who is praying. Dr. Alex Carrel writes, "The influence of prayer on the human mind and body is as demonstrable as that of secreting glands. Its results can be measured in terms of increased physical buoyancy, greater intellectual vigor, moral stamina, and a deeper understanding of the realities underlying human relationships." Deepak Chopra, Herbert Benson, Andrew Weil, and others demonstrate that prayer is healthy. But is it good for others? Can praying for others actually heal them?

Although strict scientific evidence is not yet considered conclusive on this issue, it is most certainly suggestive. Double-blind studies have indicated that people who are prayed for—whether or not they know about it—have shorter recovery periods and better results of surgery than those who are not prayed for. Cases of spontaneous unexplainable remission in cancer and other kinds of healing are most often found in patients who are surrounded by prayerful communities.

At San Francisco General Hospital, cardiologist Randy Byrd assigned patients in the coronary intensive care unit into two groups—192 were to be prayed for and 201 were not. The doctors and nurses on the unit, even the patients themselves, did not know who had been assigned to which group. Those doing the praying were scattered around the country and were only told the first name, diagnoses, and prognoses of the patients. According to the American Heart Association's journal, the prayed-for group had significantly fewer complications and fewer people in this group died than in the group that was not prayed for. Those who were not prayed for were five times more likely to develop infections requiring antibiotics and three times more likely to develop lung conditions leading to heart failure. While some recent researches have called such studies into question on methodological grounds, there does seem to be some kind of link between prayer and healing.

What about the hundreds and thousands of people who've been prayed for who haven't been healed? Haven't parents prayed for the healing of every child who has died? Don't countless prayers go unanswered every day? A hard, yet important, insight is that "No" is also an answer. Our belief that something is in our best interest does not mean that it is. Everyone can recall events and experiences that, at the time, seemed like tragedies yet which, in retrospect, appear to be blessings in disguise. And most also remember wishing, in the midst of the horrible experience, that it was not happening. Perhaps we prayed for help and wondered why our prayers were not answered. But when bad times turn out to be beneficial, we can be grateful that we were not given what we prayed for.

For example, many infertile couples who have then gone on to adopt describe how their feelings of grief and loss for the child they never birthed are inextricably mingled with an overwhelming joy that things worked out as they did. During their times of struggle they may well have prayed for a healthy pregnancy, yet looking back they realize that only the exact set of circumstances they went through could have brought them together with the adopted child they now love with all of their hearts. This realization doesn't completely take away their pain, but it does imbue it with new meaning.

There is an old Chinese story about a poor farmer who only had one broken down work horse to help him do his work. One day his horse got loose and ran away. His neighbors came around to offer their condolences on his bad luck, yet the farmer would only say, "Good luck, bad luck. It's hard to say." A week later, the horse returned, bringing with it five young stallions. Again, the neighbors convened to empathize with the farmer, this time to share their delight at his good fortune. Still, the farmer simply said, "Good luck, bad luck. It's hard to say."

The farmer's young nephew was working to tame the wild horses and, about a month later, fell and broke his leg. The neighbors came to commiserate, but still the old farmer would only reply, "Good luck, bad luck. It's hard to say." Two weeks after the accident, war was declared and every able-bodied young man was conscripted. The old farmer's young nephew was exempted because of his broken leg, so he was not involved in the battle at which every other young man from the village was killed. Good news, bad news. It's hard to say.

This is one of the reasons that spiritual teachers throughout time have suggested that prayers should not be specific, or at least should include an element of openness to unknown and unseen possibilities. Something along the lines of, "I pray for a healing of my friend's tumor or whatever is in her highest good." Many people have reported that although they experienced no physical cure, deep healing took place. It is very often difficult to know for certain what the best possible outcome of a situation is—for ourselves or for others. Sometimes the seemingly worst possible result turns out to have unimaginable gifts within it. Can we say, then, that our prayers were not answered because we did not get what we were asking for? Or should we say that they were heard and answered in a different way, that we did not get what we asked for but did get what we needed?

Ultimately, it is important to realize that we're not dealing with magic here, by which I mean that we're not engaged in an activity of obvious and predictable causality. Sometimes bad things happen to good people for no discernable reasons. If there is no "divine plan," we must accept the randomness and unfairness of life as unavoidable; if there is a plan, all traditions agree that we are in no position to know it and so we must accept the *apparent* randomness and unfairness of life as ultimately meaningful. Either way we should not ever allow ourselves to imagine that our prayers directly create specific outcomes. Theists and nontheists alike agree that it doesn't work like that.

E. Stanley Jones uses a wonderfully evocative illustration. He writes,

> Prayer is surrender—surrender to the will of God and cooperation with that will. If I throw out a boathook from the boat and catch hold of the shore and pull, do I pull the shore to me, or do I pull myself to the shore? Prayer is not pulling God to my will, but the aligning of my will to the will of God.

No prayer—even petitionary or intercessory prayer—is really about asking God to deliver this or that. Or at least it's not about expecting to get exactly what we ask for. Instead, Loving prayer is about opening our hearts and minds to the needs of others and of the world in which we live. Remarkably, it is also good for our own spirits. We "pull ourselves to the shore." Our understanding and compassion increase. Our capacity for love expands. Our attitude improves. Our ability to work for healing—in ourselves, in our relationships, in our social structures—is immeasurably strengthened.

Prayerful women and men throughout time testify that there is even more to it. Whether it's the Buddhist Kuan Yin, the Bodhisattva of Compassion who hears the cries of the world, or the Judeo-Christian God who cares for us as a mother hen watches over her brood, we are told that when we engage in Loving prayer, we are engaged with in return; that we set in motion something far beyond our own attitude adjustment, however important that might be. As with all types of prayer, keep an open mind and watch for surprises.

One final thought: When engaging in Loving prayer, don't forget yourself. It is very easy to think of this as prayer for others, yet the admonition in both the Jewish and Christian scriptures is to "love your neighbor as yourself," and to "do unto others as you would have them do unto you." In both cases we are to treat ourselves as well as we treat others or, more accurately, we are called on to treat others as well as we treat ourselves. It makes sense, then, to include our own needs when we pray for others' needs. This is not narcissistic. It's necessary.

Spontaneous and Recited Prayers

That prayer has great power which a person makes with all
his might. It makes a sour heart sweet, a sad heart merry, a
poor heart rich, a foolish heart wise, a timid heart brave, a
sick heart well, a blind heart full of sight, a cold heart ardent.
It draws down the great God into the little heart; it drives
the hungry soul up into the fullness of God; it brings together two lovers, God and the soul, in a wondrous place where
they speak much of love.

—Mechtild of Magdeburg

UNTIL NOW WE'VE BEEN examining the four basic types of
prayers—Naming, Knowing, Listening, and Loving. These can be
found under various names in all of the world's great religions.
Each has its proponents that herald it as *the* form of prayer—
there are those who say that the only kind of prayer that really
matters is that which praises the divine, for instance, and those
who argue that only prayers for others should be considered wor-
thy of our utterance. But the four types of prayer serve different
functions and none is complete in and of itself. Together, however, they can be said to constitute the "basic food groups" from
which a healthy diet of prayer can be created.

This leaves unaddressed, however, the issue of prayer styles, of
which there are two primary kinds—for our purposes let's call

them *spontaneous* and *recited*. Recited prayers are those for which someone else has composed the words, usually someone in antiquity although you may also find words that touch your heart in more recently written collections. Spontaneous prayers are those that are improvised out of the heart and mind of the person praying. Any of the four types of prayer can use either of these styles— a person can express gratitude for life's blessings in a prayer of naming with no forethought or turn to any of the great litanies that have been composed for that same purpose.

Is one style of prayer better than the other? Many say that the deepest, most profound prayers do not make use of words at all— rather they consist of what the Hebrew scriptures call "a sigh too deep for words." Still, many of us tend to be verbally oriented and if prayer is fundamentally about building relationship between the person praying and the divine, then sitting silently in one another's presence has its limitations. Assuming, then, that we're going to keep using words at least some of the time, would it be better to use the prayers of tradition or the spontaneous outpouring of our own hearts?

The best answer would be "It depends." Both approaches have their benefits and their difficulties. Both have advocates and detractors. In some ways it is like asking which art can more effectively transport a person—music or painting? There are some people for whom a clear answer is immediately evident; they have such a strong predilection for one or the other. But for many the choice depends entirely on the particular piece, mood, and personal circumstances.

One of the classic complaints about prayer is that it's all about repeating other people's words as if they were one's own. These rote recitations have everything to do with what we are supposed to be thinking and feeling while, in fact, having very little to do with what is actually happening in either our internal or external lives. Yet a great many religious traditions do expect their adherents to memorize prayers and mantras—the Jewish Psalms, the Buddhist Prajnaparamita Heart Sutra, and the Christian Our Father are only a few examples.

In the movie *The Apostle*, Robert Duvall's character, an evangelical preacher, goes up into his attic during a time of bitter setbacks in his life and yells his anger and frustration to his God. At one point he shouts, "I'm mad at ya, Lord. I love ya, but I'm mad at ya." The character was clearly praying, yet it was anything but a rote recitation. It was extremely personal and immediate. This, proponents of spontaneous prayers say, is the sign of true prayer—it is direct and intimate.

Recited prayers, of course, have the advantage that they have passed the test of time. The prayers enshrined by tradition are remembered because they have, in fact, touched people over the generations. They "work," if you will. Poor prayers are generally forgotten quickly; those that live on do so because they have been found to express some important truth or have touched people in profound ways.

Such prayers can, however, feel stilted or dated if they don't touch you. When you are trying to express heartfelt yearnings, someone else's words can seem off, not quite right. And that's one of the advantages of free-form, spontaneous prayers. You can put into words what you are experiencing as you're experiencing it. There's no intermediary. You can say what's on your mind or in your heart directly, without anything that doesn't ring true for you.

On the other hand, some people find it hard to express what's in their hearts; words fail them. Such people often find comfort in reciting the well-crafted prayers of tradition. Admirers of the Psalms of the Jewish and Christian traditions say that they express every human emotion. Those who have taken the time to memorize all 150 say that they find they have a beautiful prayer on their lips for every occasion. Not only does memorizing traditional prayers give you something to say when you may not have the words, but knowing that that same prayer has been prayed by countless others throughout the centuries can give you a feeling of kinship and belonging. You do not stand alone before the Great Mystery; you stand with all those who have also recited these words—past, present, and future.

"When you pray," Jesus cautions his followers in the Bible, "do not heap up words as do those who love to pray on the steps of the synagogue so that they might be heard by others." This is another challenge for spontaneous prayer. Just as it is possible to talk for the sake of hearing one's own voice, it is possible to pray for the sake of praying. Neither is conducive to *listening*, which is an essential element of prayer. Just as all the truly great jazz musicians know how much to pack into their solos and don't play one note too many, it is important in spontaneous prayer to give voice to what must be said and no more.

That said, getting the words "right"—whether in recited prayers from tradition or in spontaneous prayers of the heart—should never be an overriding concern. There is no magic in the words themselves. It is, rather, the attitude one brings to prayer—the honesty and authenticity, the openness and vulnerability, the courage and commitment—that is primary.

In 1886 Leo Tolstoy published a short story about a bishop on an ocean voyage who passed by a small island inhabited by three holy hermits. The bishop asked for the opportunity to go meet these men, and it was arranged. As he talked with the hermits he asked about their prayer practice and they replied, "We pray as we have always prayed—'you are three, we are three, have mercy on us.'" The bishop was horrified and proceeded to teach them a proper prayer—the Lord's Prayer as taught in the Gospel of Matthew. It took nearly all day, but as the sun was setting the hermits seemed to have the prayer fairly well memorized and the bishop returned to his ship feeling quite good about his endeavor. That evening, he awoke to the sound of shouts on deck. He went topside to see a golden glow moving toward him across the water. As it got closer, the bishop was amazed to see the three hermits, surrounded by a nearly blinding aura, running on the water. "Reverend Father," they called out, "we are terribly sorry to trouble you but soon after you left we realized that we could not remember precisely the prayer you taught us today. Please return to teach us again." The bishop did return, but to learn rather than teach.

There is one subcategory of recited prayer that deserves special attention, repetitive prayers. These are prayers that are recited for their own sake, regardless of the mood or condition of the one who is praying. The Catholic rosary is an example—the same words prayed daily by millions around the world. The meditation gathas of the Vietnamese Buddhist tradition, short phrases that accompany just about every action of a monk's day, from brushing his teeth to sitting down on his cushion to going to the bathroom, are also examples. The Muslim's recitation of the ninety-nine names of God could be in this category, as would the Greek Orthodox practice of continuously repeating what's known as the Jesus Prayer—"Lord Jesus Christ, Son of God, have mercy on me, a sinner." These prayers are recited in good times and bad, in times of hope and hopelessness.

Especially to proponents of spontaneous prayer, these repetitive prayers seem particularly problematic. Reciting other people's words might feel inauthentic but at least you can pick and choose and find words that are somewhat appropriate. The practice of repetitive prayer, though, doesn't even make an attempt to match the words to your concerns.

Of course, that's part of the point. Proponents of repetitive prayer stress that prayer is not supposed to be all about you and your concerns. It is too easy for our egos to get caught up in our praying, and repetitive prayer takes the ego out of it. The person who is praying does so not as an expression of his or her own unique self but simply out of loving obligation, simply because it is the right thing to do. The mystery of this kind of prayer is that those who regularly engage such practices say that it's amazing how personal and expressive the words become. When, for instance, one prays the rosary day in and day out, it can begin to feel like an ongoing, personal, and very pertinent conversation rather than a mere memorization drill.

There is an old acting exercise that consists of taking a sentence and seeing how many different ways it can be said: *I* love you very much. I love *you* very much. I *love* you very much. I love you *very* much. I love you very much. The words of repetitive prayers can take on a similar array of meanings depending on the mood of the person praying. The words may remain the same, but the emphasis changes with each repetition. The words become your own.

Even more, repetitive prayers are said to "sink" into a person—that is one of the reasons they are often called prayers of the heart because they move from the head to the heart. Over time, the words cease to become important at all—they are too well known—yet the movement, the rhythm of the prayer descends into you and you find that it continues to pray itself long after you think of your praying as done. The prayer becomes part of you, like the beating of your heart or the expansion and contraction of your lungs. Such an experience is only possible with a prayer that one has learned by heart, a prayer that you have said so many times that it has become part of the fabric of your living. This just isn't possible with spontaneous, and therefore unique and unrepeatable, prayers.

Repetitive prayer can also serve as a stepping stone between apophatic and katophatic forms of prayer. The benefits of wordlessness might be clear, but not everyone is comfortable in true silence. It's not easy to clear one's mind. The mind can be a voracious tiger, and these repetitive prayers, with words that one doesn't have to really think about, can be the "meat" for our verbally oriented minds. In fact, the repetition makes it virtually impossible to keep thinking about the meaning of the words. Repetitive prayer works in much the same way that the drone of a chant or the movements of a Sufi dance lull the practitioner into an altered state of consciousness.

In his book *The Breath of Life*, Episcopal priest Father Ron delBene describes a method for developing your own repetitive prayer that is as simple as choosing a name for God and naming what it is you want. He calls these *breath prayers* because each phrase is connected to the in-breath or the out-breath: Eternal Beloved / let me feel your peace. Holy of holies / I would know you. Spirit of Life / fill me. This is essentially the format used by the Orthodox Christian prayer mentioned earlier, Lord Jesus Christ, Son of God / have mercy on me, a sinner.

Developing your own breath prayer is not as simple as it sounds. The challenge is to look deeply enough to find what it is that you truly want, beneath all the other things you might feel you want or need. You might at first think you want a raise, or a better job, but go deeper and ask yourself why you want these things. You might find yourself praying, instead, for a sense of security or freedom from fear. Identify the one thing you feel the need for more than anything else, the deepest yearning of your heart and mind, and pray for that.

Likewise, the invitation is to find the name that most clearly evokes your overall sense of who or what the sacred is. Don't just pick the first name that comes to mind, or the one from tradition that feels most comfortable. Really take the time to come up with a name that encapsulates all that you think of God. When you put this most true name with your deepest need, a breath prayer has been born.

The temptation when using breath prayers—whether those of tradition or those of your own design—is to use one for a little while and then, if nothing seems to be happening or if something else pops into your mind, change to a new one. It is important to stay with one such prayer for quite some time—long enough to allow it to sink into you. If you change the prayer you are using too quickly, you will find that you've experienced all the empty repetition and none of the depth.

Neither spontaneous or recited prayers are "better." Use whichever style allows you to most fully and authentically express your deepest self—your hopes and fears, your pain and your possibilities. This might not remain consistent for you. Different life circumstances might call for different prayer styles. If all you have ever known of prayer are the words of your tradition, try praying spontaneously, as if talking with an old friend. If that is the only way you have known to pray, try taking a look at some of the prayers that have been handed down through generations of seekers. After all, even the most time-honored prayer was once the spontaneous outpouring of someone's heart!

MAKING A PRACTICE OF PRAYER

All things rest on me as pearls on a string.

—Krishna

Beads in Prayer

To use beads with a prayer, Indian or Moslem or Christian,
is to enflesh the words, make thought tangible.
—Madeleine L'Engle

BUDDHISTS CALL THEM *mala*; Muslims, *tesbih*. Eastern Orthodox
Christians use *komboloi*, Hindus use *japamala*, and Catholics, the
rosary. Whatever the name, the use of beads as a tool of prayer is
widespread, both throughout religions and throughout time.
Evidence of bead making has been found dating from at least
thirty thousand years ago. This means that before our ancestors
began painting the walls of their caves, they were making beads.

We have no way of knowing for sure whether or not these
early beads were prayer beads. Yet archaeologists and anthropol-
ogists have long surmised that early peoples attached spiritual significance to nearly everything they did and, perhaps especially,
everything they made. It seems likely, then, that these early beads
had religious meanings as well.

We do know that as far back as 3200 B.C. Egyptians were refer-
ring to beads as *sha sha*, which suggests a spiritual connotation as
sha was their word for luck. The first incontrovertible evidence of
beads used for prayer comes from Hinduism's *Arthava Veda*, written around 800 B.C., which gives detailed instructions for the use
of prayer beads. These instructions include that the beads should

not be touched with either the second finger or the whole left hand, should not be shaken or swung, and should never be dropped. The beads themselves were imbued with sacred significance.

In the West, the most familiar form of prayer beads is probably the Catholic rosary. There is archaeological evidence that at least by the late seventh century C.E. Christians were using strung beads for prayer. Fragments of a set were found in the tomb of Abbess Gertrude of Nivelles. In the eleventh century Lady Godiva, who is better known, perhaps, for her questionable taste in equestrian apparel, provides the first written record of prayer beads in Christendom; in her will she bequeathed her prayer beads to the convent she founded.

Despite early evidence of the religious use of beads, Catholic teaching is that St. Dominic, a twelfth-century monk, first saw the rosary in a vision of the Virgin Mary. The beads in the vision had the scent of roses, since they had come from her rose garden in heaven. The name rosary comes from the Latin word *rosarium*, which means "rose garden." Often rosaries are made from crushed rose petals, and the beads are often carved to look like little roses. In medieval artistic symbolism, Mary's heavenly rose garden is the counterpoint to the Garden of Eden, from which Adam and Eve are expelled. The rosary is, in a sense, a portable representation of this heavenly garden.

The traditional rosary consists of fifteen groupings of ten beads, each grouping separated by a large bead. Set prayers are recited on each bead, and each grouping represents a "mystery" in the life of Jesus and Mary. There are five "joyful mysteries" (the annunciation, visitation, nativity, presentation in the temple, and the finding of Jesus in the temple), five "sorrowful mysteries" (the agony in the garden of Gethsemane, the scourging, crowning with thorns, carrying of the cross, and the crucifixion), and five "glorious mysteries" (the resurrection, ascension, descent of the Holy Spirit, assumption, and coronation of Mary). While the various stories may not be familiar to all, even non-Catholics will probably recognize the names of the prayers that are used—for instance, *Hail Mary, Our Father, Apostle's Creed, Gloria.* The practitioner recites the Hail Mary over and over while fingering the small beads and reflecting on the spiritual gift, or mystery, of the appropriate event; the large beads separate mysteries and are for praying the Our Father. The specifics may not be widely known outside of Catholicism, but most Westerners will think of the rosary when they hear the term *prayer beads.*

Yet Christian tradition shows beads used in a variety of formulations. Abbot Paul, one of the fourth-century desert monks who fled the decadence of Egyptian society to pursue their spiritual lives in the desert, was known to begin his daily prayers by taking three hundred pebbles into his lap. He would drop one pebble to the ground as he finished each prayer. Others tied knots in ropes that they hung around their waists or necks. Eastern Orthodox Christians have sets of thirty-three, fifty, one hundred, or three hundred beads or knots in a circle connected by a cross or a tassel. Anglican prayer beads consist of twenty-eight beads in groups of seven, and in the late 1980s an Episcopal priest developed a set consisting of thirty-three beads, one for each year of Jesus' life.

Christianity is not the only religious tradition to make use of beads. The Hindu term for prayer beads is *japamala*—*mala* being the name of the beads and *japa* being the name for the practice of fingering the beads while reciting prayers. *Japamala* can be translated as "muttering beads." Traditionally, japamala are made of 108 beads, which are thought to refer to the 108 dimensions of the universe, the 108 names of the eternal female and male figures of Tara and Shiva, the 108 names for the sacred Ganges river, the 108 Upanishads, or the 108 forms of meditation! Clearly this number has deep significance. Whatever the meaning ascribed to the number, the 108 beads of the japamala are intended to help the practitioner with the recitation of her or his prayers.

The Buddhist tradition, which grew out of Hinduism in about 500 B.C., also makes use of mala consisting of 108 beads. In the Mokugenji Sutra there is a story of a king named Haruri who sought the Buddha's teaching of a simple method by which the profound wisdom of Buddhism could be shared with his people. According to the Sutra, the Buddha replied,

> King, if you want to eliminate earthly desires and to put an end to their suffering, make a circular string of 108 beads made from the seeds of the Mokugenji tree. Hold it always to yourself. Recite 'Nam Buddha–Nam Dharma–Nam Sangha.' Count one bead with each recitation.

Although the number of mala beads is the same in both Hinduism and Buddhism, the reason given for that number is different. Hinduism, as noted, draws on the cosmic significance of the number itself, while in Buddhism the number of beads refers to the number of passions to which one is striving to "put an end." In the Buddhist tradition there are six senses—sight, smell, taste, touch, hearing, and consciousness. Each sense can give rise to one of three feelings—pleasant, unpleasant, or indifferent. This gives eighteen possible combinations, each of which can further be classified as either attached to or detached from pleasure. Thus there are thirty-six basic passions, and these can occur in the past, present, or future. All the permutations taken together equal 108. (And you thought all you had to do to understand Buddhism was sit on a cushion!) Tibetan Buddhists call their beads *trengwa*, which is also the word for the purring of a cat. The droning repetition of the monks' mantra has a similar quality to that of the cat's purr and is said to bring about a similar state of bliss.

Judaism does not seem to have developed a specific prayer form for using beads, yet the prayer shawl, the *talith*, has a specific number of knots, strings, tassels, and fringes making it, in some respects, similar to prayer beads. This similarity becomes clearer when examining the passage in the Hebrew Scriptures in which the instructions to make the shawl are found. In the book of Numbers, God instructs Moses to tell the people of Israel to put fringes on their garments so that they might look on them and remember the commandments of their Lord. As we will see, other traditions substitute knotted ropes for strung beads. Since the knots, strings, tassels, and fringes of the talith are intended to help the devout to remember God's commandments, this tradition is close kin to the use of prayer beads.

The Muslim tradition makes use of beads called tashih, which consist of ninety-nine beads strung in a circle with a hundredth larger bead or tassel of silk. Traditionally there are ninety-nine attributes, or names, of Allah as well as a hundredth name that is secret. The beads provide a way for the practitioner to continually recite the holy names. By meditating on these names—All-Merciful, All-Compassionate, Source of Peace, Ever-Forgiving, All-Seeing, the Expansive, and so on—one can develop a deeper understanding of and relationship with the One who is many-named.

Prayer beads are found in a number of other traditions as well. In some Chinese Taoist sects, circles of twelve to twenty beads are used. The mantra *fu, lu, his, sou* (fortune, wealth, happiness, long life) is recited. Baha'is use a circle of ninety-five beads that has a spacer after the nineteenth; the whole circlet is joined by a larger bead. Two strings are attached to the larger bead, one with three smaller beads and one with two. Practitioners recite *Allah'u'abha*, which means "God, the most glorious," as they finger the beads. One could even include the secular use of so-called "worry beads" in a number of Latin American and African cultures as a form of prayer bead use.

The wide ranging commonality of the use of prayer beads is remarkable but unsurprising, given the world's history. Religions tend to borrow and adapt from one another. Although the world is more globalized today than it has ever been before, cultures have always crossed paths with each other and freely appropriated practices that seemed worthwhile. Christianity, for instance, borrowed from pre-Christian pagan solstice festivals when developing the rites and rituals of Christmas and Easter. Even the name *Easter* comes from the pre-Christian Germanic Goddess Oester. The use of prayer beads may well be an idea that was so useful that many who encountered them adapted them for their own needs.

This begs the questions, of course, of why anyone started using prayer beads in the first place and what makes them so useful. Perhaps Abbot Paul's use of stones is a good indication. As people developed ever more complex prayer practices, some method of keeping track was needed. After all, if you are going to lose yourself in prayer it can be all too easy to lose track of your praying. Prayer beads provide a method for remembering your prayers without much conscious effort—the bead itself is the reminder. One Japanese Buddhist prayer bead set is described as being able to help the practitioner keep track of 36,736 prayers or repetitions!

Furthermore, beads are portable. You can take them with you wherever you go and merely fingering the beads as they rest in your pocket can help bring a prayerful presence to mundane moments such as standing in line at the Department of Motor Vehicles. The human mind seems to crave a sense of setting. We often create little sacred spaces, altars—perhaps a plant, photos, a stone, a treasured gift—around our homes and work places. We have particular places where we like to engage in our spiritual practices, and most teachers encourage this. Moving into our ritual space provides a psychological nudge that helps us to shed our hectic and harried lives and settle into our prayers. Beads can be thought of as mobile altars.

Finally prayer beads have an aesthetic dimension. They have colors and shapes that are pleasing to our eyes. We feel their smooth or rough surfaces as we finger them. We hear them as they rub against one another. Beads bring more than a mere mnemonic aid to our prayers; they provide a way for us to engage all of our senses in our praying. Our eyes, ears, fingers, and even sometimes our noses are engaged, and this is no small thing. As children of the Enlightenment, Westerners often experience a deep divide between their spirituality and their physical bodies. Many of us have been taught that these two are eternally separate, yet how can we "love God with all our mind, and all our heart, and all our soul," as the Judeo-Christian tradition teaches, if we must do so without our bodies?

Unitarian Universalist minister Kenneth L. Patton writes, "Let us worship with our eyes and ears and fingertips; let us love the world through heart and mind and body.... Let us worship with the opening of all the windows of our beings, with the full outstretching of our spirits." Prayer beads provide one way for us to do just that, for they appeal to all of our senses.

The link between beads and prayer is as deep as the English language itself. The Germanic word *beth* became the Old English *gebed* which was shortened by the thirteenth century to *bede*. All of these meant *prayer*. Many, if not all, religious traditions—from ancient Hinduism to modern-day neo-Paganism—have made use of prayer beads in one form or another.

Prayer beads are a completely authentic part of the religious person's repertoire. A practice based on beads is based on one of the oldest tools in humanity's quest for connection and meaning. There is no one right format or formula for using prayer beads. Versions and variations abound, so developing a new practice is merely a continuation of this age-old process of evolution and adaptation.

A Modern Prayer Bead Practice

> The moment you wake up each morning, all your wishes and hopes for the day rush at you like wild animals. And the first job each morning consists in shoving it all back, in listening to that other voice, taking that other point of view, letting that other, larger, stronger, quieter life come flowing in.
>
> —C. S. Lewis

THE FOUR TYPES OF PRAYER, Naming, Knowing, Listening, and Loving, can be brought together into a single prayer bead practice that incorporates both the spontaneous and recited styles as well. Although every major religious tradition has some form of prayer bead practice, many people today find these practices inaccessible or unfulfilling. For one thing, many prayer bead practices are so intimately intertwined with the particular forms and flavors of specific religious traditions that people outside of those traditions can feel excluded. How, for instance, can someone who is not versed in or appreciative of the mysteries of the life of Mary find meaning in the Catholic rosary? Those who are familiar with the stories and metaphors of the life of Jesus' mother can indeed find great power and depth in this practice; those who are unfamiliar often find in it nothing more than a rote recitation of meaning-less words. The same dichotomy can be experienced whenever insiders and outsiders approach the prayer practices developed within any one of the world's great religions.

A second difficulty many encounter is that most prayer bead practices are focused on one of the four major prayer types; they are to be used as aids in the recitation of the names of the divine, for instance, or to assist in keeping track of the people whose concerns one is holding in prayer. These practices, then, generally have one primary intention, and toward those specific ends they can be extremely valuable. Yet many people today are seeking a more holistic approach to their spiritual quest and looking for a practice that embraces the totality of our spiritual experiences while remaining flexible enough to respond to changing circumstances, desires, and needs.

This modern prayer bead practice incorporates all four of the prayer types as stages on a journey of prayer, and since the beads are strung in a circle it does not elevate one type above any other. The circularity of the practice is also reflective of the circularity of the spiritual path; one takes these steps over and over with each being just another step on a never ending journey. It can be instructive to remember that during the forty years following his enlightenment experience Siddhartha, the Buddha, continued to meditate every day; Jesus is remembered as regularly going off to a quiet place to pray even after God declares him "my beloved in whom I am well pleased." One is never finished with the spiritual journey. One never arrives.

This bead set for this practice makes use of twenty-eight beads—a large centering bead, four medium-sized beads (for the four types of prayer), and twenty-three small beads (to be used primarily for breath prayers). Since this is a modern, non-denominational practice, you will not find beads ready-made in this configuration. You will have to make them yourself. Any good bead or craft store can help you find the beads you need and teach you how to string them together. Even the craft-challenged should try to string their own prayer beads, as the process itself can be a spiritual exercise. Imbue the beads with the energy of your intention for this practice as you string them—imagine yourself using them, see yourself centering more deeply into the depths of your life, visualize the outcome you are hoping for in adopting a new spiritual practice.

You can go to a local bead store and purchase the beads you will need. If you've never been to such a place, you'll be amazed at the variety available to you: precious and semi-precious stones, wooden beads, simple balls, carved and faceted shapes, in more colors than in the rainbow. Take your time and choose beads that speak to you. Try to find beads that look and feel appealing and that would inspire you to pick them up and use them. People have made prayer beads that look as formal and delicate as the finest Catholic rosary, or as jumbled and idiosyncratic as a charm bracelet.

You can also make your own beads. Buy a self-drying modeling clay or a clay that can be hardened in the oven (like Sculpy). Roll balls in the sizes and shapes you want, and then stick a toothpick through them to make a hole. Leave the toothpick in while the balls dry so that the holes won't close up as the clay shrinks. You can then paint your beads if you like, or leave them the plain color of the clay.

If you really want to know that your beads are wholly your own, you can make your own clay: The simplest method is to combine flour, salt, and water to make a paste. You can add dried rose petals—traditional in the making of the Catholic rosary—or other dried flowers or herbs, making sure that they are ground to powder. Mix all of the ingredients and then form the beads as mentioned above. One monastery that specializes in making rosaries claims that the smell of the dried roses will linger on the beads for up to fifty years!

Whether you are buying or making your own beads, string them in the following order: large bead (Centering), four small beads (Entering In), first medium bead (Naming), five small beads (Breath Prayer), second medium bead (Knowing), five small beads (Breath Prayer), third medium bead (Listening), five small beads (Breath Prayer), fourth medium bead (Loving), and four small beads (Returning). Connect the cord back to the original large bead, completing the circle.

The beads are strung in a circle to remind us that this is not a linear journey nor a one-time-only event; we end where we began, and then we begin again. As the poet T.S. Eliot writes, "And the end of all our exploring / will be to arrive at where we started / and know the place for the first time." This prayer bead practice is designed to help weave together the types or stages of prayer experience, facilitating this journey into the innermost depths of one's own life, into the depths of Life itself, yet as we've noted it is a journey that will never be finished. We must engage it again and again.

Once you have your own set of prayer beads, slowly begin to work your way through the beads, holding one at a time. Start with the largest one.

Centering: The large bead is for *Centering* yourself in preparation for the journey. To "be still and know that I am God," can be tremendously difficult in our hectic and harried lives. The Taoist sage Lao-tzu asked, "Do you have the patience to wait until the mud settles and the water clears on its own?" Few of us do. Most of us charge ahead, barreling into the next moment, running on the adrenaline and the momentum of the last. This bead is an antidote. It encourages you to stop before taking the first step of this journey.

Think of it as if you are standing at the threshold of a temple or a serene woodland glade. Pause a moment before entering. Allow your eyes to adjust to the different lighting within. Allow your body, your mind, to acclimate to a new and more peaceful rhythm. Breathe in and out several times, calming the body and quieting the mind.

You might choose to sing a favorite hymn, or recite a favorite preparatory prayer. On Sacred Space, a web site run by Irish Jesuits, there is a beautiful preparatory prayer:

> Lord, I so wish to prepare well for this time. I want to make
> all of me ready and attentive and available to you. Please

help me to clarify and purify my intentions. I have so many contradictory desires. I get so preoccupied with things that don't really matter or last. I know that if I give you my heart, whatever I do will follow my new heart. In all that I am today, all that I try to do, all my encounters, reflections— even my frustrations and failings—and especially in this time of prayer, in all of this may I place my life in your hands. Lord, I am yours. Make of me what you will. Amen.

Alternatively, you could repeat a Buddhist meditation gatha such as the one popularized by the Vietnamese monk Thich Nhat Hanh, "Breathing in, I relax body and mind. Breathing out, I smile. Dwelling in the present moment I realize this is the only moment." You might choose to gaze at a candle or an icon, or you might choose to simply sit in silence. Whatever helps you to shed the weight and rush of the day is right; whatever helps you to feel that you're entering into a sacred time and space—a bubble in the hustle and bustle of your life—is right. When you feel ready, move on.

Entering In: The four small beads at the beginning of the prayer circle provide a way to enter into the journey of prayer. With each bead you might recite one of the four Bodhisattva vows of Zen Buddhism—"Sentient beings are numberless, I vow to save them. Desires are inexhaustible, I vow to put an end to them. The Dharmas are countless, I vow to master them. The Buddha Way is unattainable, I vow to attain it."

You might call on the spirits of Earth, Air, Fire, and Water, or call upon the four directions of North, South, East, and West. You could say a favorite four-line poem, or you could create your own entering prayer. For instance:

> Open my eyes, that I might see your face in everyone I meet. Open my ears, that I might hear your voice in whatever forms it takes. Open my hands, that I might freely give whatever is mine to share. Open my heart, that I might live and love more fully in you—you who created me, you who redeemed me, and you who sustain me.

These beads are like the warm-up period in an aerobics class or the time of stretching before a long run. Make no mistake—a spiritual practice seriously undertaken is a real workout. Easing into it is strongly recommended if you want to avoid cramps.

What are these "cramps"? Most of us live our day-to-day lives trying to maximize our control of external situations, yet within the time of prayer we need to let go of control. Moving too quickly into prayer can mean that we bring our normal assumptions and attitudes with us and thus undermine the very thing we're trying to do. We may hold on too tight, or push to hard, trying to accomplish and attain when we should really be trying to let go and relax into life's own flow. We might strive to be in charge of our prayer time—as we try to be in charge of most everything else around us—forgetting the admonition of the Unitarian Universalist minister Barbara Merritt, "Whether or not we believe in God, we must recognize that we ourselves are not God."

The four beads for Entering In allow us to move slowly into our prayer which should help us to avoid such problems.

Naming: The first medium-sized bead is for Naming the Holy. This is your chance to name the Sacred, to give voice to what you consider Holy or where you have felt the Divine in your life. You might use the names of Gods and Goddesses from the world's religions, or you might make up your own invocation. It can be as simple as, "Great and Gracious God, known by many names yet by no Name fully known . . . ," or as complex as:

> Ancient and Ageless Spirit: Mother and Father of All; Gods and Goddess of old; all Buddhas throughout space and time; Spirits, Saints, and Sages; Wise Women and Men . . . (etc.)"

If you prefer not to imagine the Divine as personal, you could call up the attributes that you ascribe to the Sacred, or name whatever feeds your soul; this is your opportunity to give name to what you feel to be holy and sacred. Hindus often tell the story of a woman who went to the priest in her village and confessed that she could not believe in God. "What is it that gives you the most joy?"

the priest asked. "What gives your life meaning and purpose?" "My children," she replied. "Then whenever the prayers speak of God," the priest advised, "think of your children." This bead provides the opportunity for you to reflect on and name that which gives you the most joy and that gives your life meaning and purpose.

It is also the place for you to lift up all for which you are thankful at this moment, all the blessings and miracles in your life, all the joy in your living. Whichever approach you take—naming the sacred or counting your blessings—take your time. Most of us spend far more time reflecting on what's wrong in our lives than we do in noticing the many blessings and miracles around us. It would do us all well to spend more time noting the latter.

Knowing: The second medium-sized bead is for knowing yourself. As Socrates said, "The unexamined life is not worth living." With the Knowing bead you have an opportunity to reflect on your life as it is today, to recognize those places that call for reconciliation and atonement. We are each a mixture of saint and sinner, and this stop on our journey is an opportunity to see and know yourself in all your subtle shadings. This is not a call for guilt or self-criticism but for honest self-appraisal. To use the language of the Twelve Step Movement, this is the opportunity to take a "fearless moral inventory." Unless we acknowledge our faults and failings we can do nothing about overcoming them. Unless we know ourselves fully—in all our light and shadow—we may fear that there are parts of who we are that are unacceptable. Prayer demands of us that we show up with our whole—and holy— selves. This bead encourages that, and allows us to move on. Here, too, take your time, not in recrimination but in honest assessment.

Listening: The third medium-sized bead calls you to sit back and *Listen*; it is a place for revelation, not discourse. Again, this is a time to be still. A traditional misunderstanding of prayer is that it is all about talking to God. True prayer is at least as much about listening to the holy "voice of quiet stillness" as it is about using our own voices. As Thomas Keating says, "We may think of prayer as thoughts or feelings expressed in words. But this is only one expression. Contemplative prayer is the opening of mind and heart—our whole being—to God, the Ultimate Mystery, beyond thoughts, words, and emotions."

This bead creates a space to be still and listen to the Divine spark, the Buddha-nature, the inner wisdom that is inherent in us all. Here, again, you may meditate silently; gaze on an icon, statue, or mandala; or reflectively read scripture, practicing what is known as *lectio divina*. The Shalem Institute for Spiritual Formation speaks of this type of prayer as "getting ourselves out of the way so that God can pray in us."

Loving: The final medium-sized bead helps us to follow prayer's natural movement toward an ever widening concern for the wider world. Here we lift up those we know (and those we don't) whose lives have pain and need. Hold them in your consciousness, bring them to your awareness. As said earlier, we do not pray so that God knows about people's needs; we pray to make sure we know. You could have a list of people who you feel are in need of prayer, and repeat their names as you visualize them. You could also sit quietly and see who comes into your mind. However you choose to do it, this bead is an invitation to extend your practice beyond yourself to the world around you.

Returning: The four beads that lead from the Loving bead back to the Centering bead are a way of returning to the world, mirroring the four beads used to Enter In. The Zen tradition explicitly faces the need to re-enter the world, recognizing that the peace and tranquility found in meditation can be seductive and can lure people from real living. It is "in the dust of the marketplace" rather than "on top of the mountain" that one's meditation is fully realized. What was put down at the beginning of this journey must be picked up again. Life must be re-engaged. So release the Directions, repeat your vows, or say your entering prayer again. Since the beads form a circle, this path of return is also a re-entry; the world to which we return is not quite the same as the one we left.

Breath Prayers: What of the five small beads that separate each of the medium-sized beads? They provide a link between the stages of the journey. With each of these beads you may use a breath prayer, a two-line phrase that is said in rhythm with the in- and out-breaths: for example, *Breathing in I develop calm and equanimity. Breathing out I find peace and joy, Lord Jesus Christ. Have mercy on me, Great Mystery. I seek to know.* Many traditions extol the virtues of repetitive, set prayers over which the practitioner has no control; this kind of praying removes any ego-involvement in the composition process, preventing you from getting caught up in eloquent or flowery phrases. Many today look down on such a practice as too formal or ritualistic, but it has great power. Try it and see.

Centering, Naming, Knowing, Listening, and Loving—this is the journey of this prayer practice: Taking the time to find a quiet place in your life, setting in front of your awareness the Holy and Sacred miracle of life, seeing yourself within that reality as full and whole, tuning your senses to hear inner wisdom, and then turning your attention to the needs within and around you.

Whether you are Buddhist, Baptist, or Bah'ai, this pattern can be embellished with specifics from your faith tradition. You can utilize traditional intercessory prayers while fingering the Loving bead if you are a Catholic, for instance, or you can speak to the Bodhisattva Kuan Yin—"she who hears the cries of the world"— if you are Buddhist. If you have no particular faith tradition of your own, you can simply see it as a time to allow the cares and concerns of life to come more fully into your consciousness. This practice does not demand any one set of images and ideas. Rather, it provides a framework within which you can find out for yourself what is present in the depth of your life.

A Practice of Your Own

I will spare you any description of the way in which one can
make time: I will only say that if we try to waste a little less
of it, there will be more of it. If we use crumbs of wasted
time to try to build short moments for recollection and
prayer, we may discover that there is quite a lot of it.

— Anthony Bloom

THE SPECIFIC PRAYER BEAD practice just described was developed
with an eye toward balance—raising up what you are thankful for
as well as what you know needs work, looking at your own wants
and needs while also bringing to mind the needs of others, naming the holy and sacred dimensions of life as you know them and
listening to what life will say to you. With its mixture of free,
spontaneous prayer and set, repetitive prayer, this practice aims at
providing a fully rounded experience to the practitioner. Think of
it as a complete circuit program for the spirit, incorporating every
major muscle group and the cardiovascular system, stretching
and strength training. Those who have made and used a set of
beads in this way report that it has been an exciting method to
bring disciplined prayer back into their lives, finding it to be flexible enough to hold the varied spiritual influences which are part
of so many of us today.

The entire practice can take anywhere from thirty to sixty

minutes. You can, of course, shorten or lengthen it depending on available time and your own sense of need. You can carry your beads with you wherever you go and may find yourself fingering them while on line or in a meeting. Moments that, in the past, would have been a source of frustration now become an opportunity for going deeper; life's little irritations become invitations. This, as noted earlier, is one of the benefits of the tactile quality of prayer beads—simply touching them can have an affect akin to listening to soothing music in a scented sanctuary. M. Basil Pennington, one of the creators of Centering Prayer, wrote in *Praying by Hand*,

> Fingering beads often helps our concentration. This is one of their greater benefits. While they occupy and integrate our external senses into our prayer, our mind is left freer to attend to its own level of reality. . . . Even when the rational mind is occupied in conversation or some other simple task, beads can support the spirit in its course of prayer. Deliberately holding the beads can in itself be the prayer . . .

You can do portions of the prayer while you sit in traffic or stand in line—touching the Centering bead to center yourself, for instance, or using the Loving bead to move you out of self-centeredness. At the same time, though, you can also just run the beads through your fingers and bring to mind the attitude of prayerfulness that you are cultivating during your times of daily practice.

Similarly, you can expand this practice, taking a whole day to move through its stations using the medium-sized beads as break points, picking up at a later time where you'd left off—e.g., Centering when you wake up, Naming after breakfast, Knowing at lunchtime, Listening in mid-afternoon, and Loving in the evening. In this way you let the rhythm of the prayers inform the rhythm of your day.

At least once a week you should try taking the entire journey. It is important to remember that these different approaches and styles of prayer are interconnected, are part of a whole, each feeding the others. It can be quite powerful to notice—to observe and experience—the transformational flow of your emotions as you move through the various kinds of prayer. You'll no longer have to take someone else's word for the fact that our lives are made up of intertwined joy and sorrow, for you'll have felt both in the course of your praying. You'll see your strengths and weaknesses in equal measure and, so, be able to accept your whole—and holy—self.

Ideally, we would be able to create a daily discipline of prayer. Someone once said that wise people do not begin to sew their parachutes as they are jumping out of a plane. The same can be said of our prayer life. We ought not begin trying to pray in our time of greatest spiritual need. The phrase spiritual practice implies something done with regularity and intention, something we return to again and again. The related phrase—*spiritual discipline*—is not much in favor these days, because many people see in it a sense of being forced, or rigidity, or lifelessness. There is much in it though that we would do well to reclaim.

You can make sounds on a musical instrument playing it from time to time, whenever the mood strikes. You can learn to make music if your playing has an element of discipline, becomes a practice. Cellist Pablo Casals, one of the most accomplished musicians in recent history, continued his discipline of practicing five to six hours every day long past the time when it was clear that he had attained the highest levels of accomplishment. A friend once asked him why he continued to practice at the age of ninety-three. "I keep practicing," Casals replied, "because I think I'm beginning to make some progress." On the day he died at ninety-six, his practice consisted of playing scales.

You are not alone if your reaction to this story is mixed. On the one hand it can reassure us that even those who've apparently "made it" still have work to do, still have lessons to learn, still have room for improvement. This can be seen, too, in the stories of Jesus making regular time for prayer and Siddhartha continuing to meditate daily even after his enlightenment. If enlightened masters and accomplished artists still have things to learn and the need to practice their scales, practicing is good for us as well. In that way, it is a comfort.

On the other hand, these lessons also tell us that there'll always be work to do, that we'll never finish, and that once we start off on the spiritual journey with diligence and discipline there'll be no turning back. None of us ever gets there; our destination is the journey itself. That can be daunting. Especially because one of the major hurdles that many people face when taking up a spiritual practice is the sense that this is one more thing to fail at. The memory of diets broken and regimens of physical exercise forgotten can loom large. We know how many things we've begun and not finished; we don't want our prayer beads to end up gathering dust along with our musical instruments, treadmills, and cookbooks.

In his book *Space for God*, Don Postema writes of a conversation he has with the abbot of a monastery where he has been on a four-day retreat. He explains how much he wants to keep to the regularity of prayer he has experienced at the monastery—where the monks gather seven times a day for services of prayer and worship. He asks the abbot how he can make prayer as much a priority out in the demanding and distracting "real world" as it had been in the quiet stillness of the monastery.

Many of us face this same question. We want to deepen our lives, we want to connect with the source of all that is, we want to develop an attitude of prayerfulness in our living, yet the kids are crying, the bills need to be paid, we're staying overtime at work, and so on. In our all-too-often hectic lives there are a thousand and one ways for us to be distracted and diverted, kidnapped from our attentiveness. So what advice did Postema get? The abbot said simply, "First you have to want to pray."

So that's the first thing. You must decide that you really want to do this. Make it a conscious decision. Decide on a time and place for your praying so that you know when and where it fits into your life. In the beginning it might make sense to actually write it into your calendar, like anything else you want to make sure you attend to on a regular basis. Postema also tells of the change that occurred in his own prayer life when the entry on his calendar changed from "time for prayer" to "appointment with God." The former was apparently too easy to let slip while "appointment with God" was harder to ignore. Perhaps that is because an appointment involves a relationship with another person while a task to be done can often be put off without any real trouble. You might need to find your own language to express the same sense of urgency Postema found in his daily appointment with God—Meeting With My True Self, or Appointment with Life might work for you. If you want to make a spiritual practice a regular part of your life you must set aside the time for it.

Does it matter when? For many people, first thing in the morning is ideal—it sets the tone for the day. Yet the morning is often when we're getting the kids up and dressed, the dog walked, lunches made, and the family out the door. So what about taking time when you first arrive at work? Or during your lunch hour? Perhaps stopping somewhere on the drive home to spend a little time in prayer? Look at the rhythms of your day as it is—not as you wish it was—and see where you can naturally create an oasis for your spiritual practice. If you're honest with yourself about the demands of your day you stand a much better chance of actually making a schedule that works.

Most teachers say that it's important to set aside the same time each day, as this increases the likelihood that you'll remember and not inadvertently schedule something over your prayer time. It also creates a sense of internal expectation. Just as, when you were in elementary school, you could sense with your body and your mind the coming of the final bell, so too you can come to anticipate the coming of your prayer time. You'll start getting ready for it even before you sit down to begin. This doesn't mean, of course, that you can't or shouldn't pray at other times. Of course you should! The contemplative ideal, in every tradition, has always been to turn one's entire life into a time of prayer. But setting aside a particular time for your practice increases the like-lihood that you will, in fact, pray at some point in your day. Remember the complaint of the apostle Paul in the Christian New Testament—he found that he was constantly doing the things he didn't want to do and was rarely doing the things he did. Apparently, the human experience hasn't changed all that much in two thousand years. Setting aside a specific time to pray improves the odds that you will actually pray.

If establishing a regular time for our prayers is the first thing we must do to make a practice of prayer, the second is to be gentle with yourself. A prayer ascribed to Lord Jacob Astley sums it up well: "O Lord! thou knowest how busy I must be this day: if I forget thee, do not thou forget me." The gentle monk known to us as Brother Lawrence, looking back at his sixty years of spiritual practice, wrote that it was as hard in the beginning to do his practice as it was now not to do it. There is no denying that a regular spiritual practice is difficult to maintain, especially in such a fast paced and secularized culture. The former allows little time for prayer and meditation and the latter provides little encouragement or support.

One insight from Eastern meditation may be helpful. The prac-tice of meditation is not really about establishing inner stillness; it is about making the decision to establish inner stillness. In classic Zen meditation, every time you notice that you have become dis-tracted, you choose then and there to simply return to your prac-tice. No recriminations. No condemnation. Just the gentle recognition that you've become distracted, and the decision to return. It is this three part movement—getting distracted, noticing the distraction, and deciding to let the distraction go and to return—that is, in fact, the practice of meditation. The moments of stillness are one of meditation's byproducts, not the practice itself.

This insight can be applied to the practice of establishing a practice. Each time you notice that it's been a while since the last time you prayed, simply decide then and there to begin praying again. No recriminations. No condemnation. Just the gentle recog-nition that you've become distracted, and the decision to return.

This is, in fact, the way you make of your life a spiritual practice—observing on a macro level the same three-part movement that you observe in your time of discipline. Whether your time frame is moment to moment or day to day, you'll see the same pattern of getting distracted, noticing the distraction, and deciding to the let the distractions go so that you may return to your practice.

Many people get frustrated and feel themselves to be failures when they find that they are unable to establish—and maintain—a regular spiritual practice. But this on again/off again, ebb and flow movement is a normal, integral part of the practice. That's why it's practice and not performance! The awareness of God's love, the sense of communing with life at its deepest levels, the feeling that "I am inseparably this and that, and this and that are I"—these things are byproducts of the practice, not the practice itself. The true activity in any spiritual practice is this training of oneself to recognize when we are being distracted by what Thoreau called "that which is not life" and the strengthening of our resolve to live only what is.

The sixteenth-century reformer Martin Luther was known to keep a practice of praying for an hour each day. Someone asked him what happened when he got too busy to spare that hour. Luther replied that on such days he prayed for two hours. This may seem absurd and, yet, it is advice that you can find across traditions and times. If your days have gotten so full that you do not have time to care for your soul, then something is out of kilter. Making an even more concerted effort than usual may well be called for to reestablish some kind of balance.

Even more practically, though, it should be pointed out that when we lose our ability to center ourselves and allow our lives to spin out of control we become increasingly ineffective in all aspects of our daily living. We not only feel but actually are being pushed and pulled by circumstances in a way that no longer allows any kind of conscious and creative response. We lose our ability to distinguish between the important and the merely urgent. And, so, we feel (and are!) overwhelmed.

Think of overworked employees who have been putting in massive amounts of overtime to get a project completed. The more tired they become, the less clear their thinking, the slower their memory snaps into gear, the less efficient they become all around. These employees should stop and take a rest—not out of laziness or disinterest but as an investment in future productivity. The thirty minutes or so they spend sleeping could well make the work time that follows it so much more productive that the "missing" time is hardly missed at all. Far from being wasted effort, the intentional time out makes the time back in less wasted.

So it is with our prayer lives. When our lives get so full that we can't take time to tend to our spirits, it is just common sense that we cannot be operating at our best. We will be cut off from one of the primary sources of our strength, wisdom, and compassion. Unless we reestablish that connection, we will become increasingly alienated from our own lives and living. Taking the time then—literally, taking back the time, reclaiming it—is actually a healthy investment in our own wholeness.

We need not, however, always follow Luther's advice and double our normally allotted time. We can take a moment to pause, finger the beads in our pocket, take a look at the world around us, and say, "Thank you." As Meister Eckhart says, just that will be sufficient.

PRAY LIKE THIS

Let me seek you in my desire,

Let me desire you in my seeking.

Let me find you by loving you,

Let me love you when I find you.

—St. Anselm

The Lord's Prayer

Our Father, who art in heaven, hallowed be Thy name.
Thy kingdom come, Thy will be done on earth as it is in
    heaven.
Give us this day our daily bread,
and forgive us our trespasses as we forgive those who
    trespass against us.
Lead us not into temptation, but deliver us from evil
for Thine is the kingdom and the power and the glory
    forever.

BOTH THE GOSPELS OF MATTHEW and Luke record an incident in which Jesus' friends ask him to teach them how to pray. His response in both cases is to offer an example—"Pray like this," he says—and then he goes on to show them how to do it. The words recorded in the two Gospels are not exactly the same, but each would be recognized as a variation of what is known today as "the Lord's prayer."

Generations have recited these words, individually and in groups, as though the words themselves were sacred. In fact, in the Catholic tradition it was once taught that these were sacred words, fit only for those who were members of the "Body of Christ," since Jesus had passed them on to his disciples only and not to the multitudes.

Neil Douglas-Klotz, in *Prayers of the Cosmos*, translated the Lord's Prayer from English back into Aramaic—the language that Jesus probably spoke—and then back into English. He points out that Aramaic is rich and subtle and full of nuance, and then offers over half a dozen wildly different yet equally valid possible translations for each of the phrases in this prayer. For instance, according to Douglas-Klotz, the first line could be read as any one of these:

> O Birther! Father-Mother of the Cosmos, you create all that moves in light.

> Radiant One: You shine within us, outside us—even darkness shines—when we remember.

> Wordless Action, Silent Potency—where ears and eyes awaken, there heaven comes.

If the Aramaic original could have so many differing English translations, how can we be certain which sacred words are *the* sacred words?

We need to remember, though, that the stories that have come to us about this prayer indicate that Jesus was not too interested in his disciples getting the words right. He is remembered as saying, "pray *like* this," not, "pray *this*." Those words that have been mumbled and memorized by millions were never intended to become revered any more than the scales and exercises given by a musician to her students are meant to be enshrined. Rather, they are tools to help the student learn to play—or pray—on his or her own. In that spirit, let's look at the Our Father as a teaching tool for composing a prayer, so that we can build our own prayer upon its structure.

Our Father, who art in heaven,

Much has been made of the fact that Jesus used the Aramaic word *ābbā*, to begin this prayer. This term is much more intimate than the traditional *ābēnû malkēnû*, which was the most common synagogue invocation during Jesus' day. *Ābēnû malkēnû* translates as "our Father, our King," whereas *abbā* is more like our "Daddy," a term of intimate endearment. This word choice communicates an understanding of the relationship with the sacred that Jesus knew and that he wished for his friends—one that is close and personal.

This prayer begins with an identification of that to which the prayer is addressed—in this case, "Daddy." One could equally well begin a prayer with "Mommy," or "Source of all that Is," or "Innermost Wisdom"—what matters is that you begin with a salutation, addressing the prayer to the sacred in some way. This particular salutation establishes that this is not the prayer of an individual but of a community. Although taught in the context of a discourse on individual prayer, this is not "My Father" who is being addressed, but "Our Father." It has been said that there are no individual Christians, because all are linked in the community of the "body of Christ."

This is not unique to Christianity. Even as apparently individualistic a religion as Buddhism reveres the community—the *sangha*—as one of the primary values. It may be true, as Walt Whitman says, that no one can walk your road for you, but that doesn't mean that we need walk alone. The world's major religions emphasize the essential importance of community. Unitarian Universalist minister Mark Morrison-Reed writes, "The central task of the religious community is to unveil the bonds that bind each to all." The form of prayer taught by Jesus teaches us that even when we pray as individuals we are doing so in the context of community.

What name would you give the sacred? What would feel like an authentic address for your prayer?

hallowed be Thy name,
Thy kingdom come,
Thy will be done on earth as it is in heaven.

After the opening invocation, this prayer moves on to two units of three requests. The first three focus on God. Despite the intimacy with which the prayer begins, the first of these reinforces the "otherness" and superiority of God: "hallowed be Thy name." To the first century Jewish mind, a name was a representation of the essence and fundamental character of a thing; therefore, this phrase really means something along the line of "May you be honored for being the Holy One you are." These three requests follow on the identification of God as *ābbā*—Daddy—with the seemingly contradictory recognition of God as the Holy One above all others. However, in just these few words, Jesus sums up what it has taken theologians thousands of pages to describe— that God is at once both *immanent* (closer than our own breathing) and *transcendent* (far beyond our comprehension).

The prayer moves from the opening salutation to a three-part statement of the prayer's intentions with regards to the sacred: The person praying desires that the holy be recognized as such, that the sacred and the secular move into closer alignment, and that, in fact, the separations between these two be blotted out until everything is known as holy and whole.

What are your hopes with regard to the sacred dimensions of life? How would you continue this prayer, not only in your own words but in your own intentions?

Give us this day our daily bread,
and forgive us our trespasses as we forgive those who trespass against us.
Lead us not into temptation, but deliver us from evil

The prayer then moves on to the second set of three requests, and these are focused on the needs of the person praying. Scholars debate whether the reference to "daily bread" is literal or figurative. As the latter, they note that the word we translate as "bread" was also an idiomatic way of talking about spiritual teaching and, after all, the Gospel of John and Christian tradition refer to Jesus himself as "the bread of life." This, then, could be a strictly spiritual request.

On the other hand, the other two elements in this set would most certainly have been understood as being literal and practical needs in the first-century Jewish mind. To be forgiven one's sins (the root meaning of the translations that read "trespasses" or "debts") would be of paramount importance. In the High Holy Day traditions of Rosh Hashanah and Yom Kippur Jews are taught that without forgiveness their names will be erased from God's Book of Life and forever separated from the Divine. And the request to be freed from temptation—or "testing"—would likewise have had immediate and literal interpretations.

So it makes sense to think that the request for "daily bread" is also a literal request. And that means that this prayer can be seen as an expression of Jesus' teaching from the Sermon on the Mount about not being anxious about what you will eat or drink, and "letting the days own worries be enough for the day." This section of the prayer can be understood as a reflection of the belief that one should turn to God not just for spiritual but for material needs as well. Note that here, too, the request is not for "my bread" or forgiveness for "me." Petitions for "our daily bread" and the forgiveness of "our trespasses" again underscore the importance of community.

What real needs do you feel, both material and spiritual? How would you phrase these needs?

for thine is the kingdom and the power and the glory forever.

Many scholars believe that this was not part of the original prayer but, rather, a later editorial addition since there are at least ten different endings among the extant ancient manuscripts, and the oldest and most authoritative do not include this last line.

Try reading the version of this prayer found in Luke 11—the language feels choppy and abrupt. Then compare it to the version in Matthew 6, which is the version most often used by Christians. Original or not, these final words provide a benediction, a flowing way to bring the prayer to a close.

What seems to you to be an appropriate way to bring a prayer to an end? Don't just mimic the words you've heard in the past; try to find your own.

If we strip this prayer of its content to expose its underlying structure, we find something like the following:

Begin with a salutation.
State your intentions regarding the sacred.
State your requests regarding yourself.
Bring the prayer to a close.

Using this format, compose a prayer that reflects your situation and your understandings. For example:

O Spirit that dwells within us all—may you be known and loved. May your insight guide us, may your compassion fill us, until this world is holy and whole. May we receive the things we most need for body and soul, and may we never stray from our heart's true path. Until the sun burns out and stars grow cold. Amen.

The Twenty-Third Psalm

The Lord is my shepherd, I shall not be in want. He makes me lie down in green pastures, he leads me beside quiet waters, he restores my soul. He guides me in paths of righteousness for his name's sake. Even though I walk through the valley of the shadow of death, I will fear no evil, for you are with me; your rod and your staff, they comfort me. You prepare a table before me in the presence of my enemies. You anoint my head with oil; my cup overflows. Surely goodness and love will follow me all the days of my life, and I will dwell in the house of the Lord forever.

ONE OF THE BEST KNOWN PRAYERS of the Jewish and Christian traditions is the Twenty-Third Psalm. It is quite possibly the most familiar passage in the Bible to most people. Many nursing home chaplains can attest to the power of this prayer for those in need of comfort. It is not at all uncommon for a roomful of people who only moments before had seemed lost in their own worlds suddenly to spark to life, robustly reciting these beloved words, often in the old language of the King James version.

Before looking at the prayer in detail, it is important to note its juxtaposition with the Twenty-Second Psalm, which casts it in a particular context.

The Twenty-Second Psalm is the keening lament of a person

in pain: "My God, my God, why have you forsaken me? . . . I am a worm, and not a human; scorned by others . . . all my bones are out of joint; my heart is like wax . . . melted within me; my mouth is dried up . . . my hands and feet have shriveled . . . ." It is one of the classic psalms of despair, giving voice to a sense of agony and hopelessness. Many people are surprised to find such a raw expression of despair in the Bible, thinking that prayer is always supposed to express positive feeling and gratitude to God for all things. Yet the Twenty-Second is one of many psalms that give voice to these kinds of angry and agonized emotions and experiences.

The Twenty-Second Psalm can be placed in the narrative of the Hebrew scriptures during the time when David, traditionally considered the author of the Psalms, is on the run from the forces of King Saul. Life as he's known it has been turned upside down. Only recently David has been Saul's closest confidant, but a false accusation has changed all of that. Once in a place of power and privilege, David now knows no safety. Accustomed to life in the palace, he is now literally living in caves. We can imagine David's sense of betrayal and injustice, not to mention fear and hopelessness, and it is from the depth of such despair that this prayer emerges.

Like nearly all the Psalms, the Twenty-Second ends on a note of hope and faith, but in this case it is there only by sheer force of will. The psalmist declares that even though nothing in his current life experience gives him any reason to continue to have faith in God, he will continue to do so because he knows the stories of how God has helped his people in the past. On the basis of those stories, he will continue to believe. In other words, he'll maintain his faith out of sheer stubbornness. His faith is part of who he is— part of his identity as a Jew—and he will willfully maintain it even in the face of external circumstances that seem to contradict it.

The Twenty-Third Psalm, on the other hand, clearly describes a belief born out of experience. It is written by someone who knows firsthand how God can move in a person's life. In effect, the psalmist writes, "I believe because I have reason to." When the Twenty-Second and Twenty-Third Psalms are read together, the story emerges of a person who, from the depths of despair, holds on to faith in God by force of will and then has that stubbornness confirmed when life itself changes for him. We can almost hear the surprised relief in the first line: "Well, what do you know? The Lord *is* my shepherd after all."

Let's, now, turn our attention to the form of the Twenty-Third Psalm.

The Lord is my shepherd

The prayer begins by establishing a metaphor—God is like a shepherd—and since many people earned their living as shepherds at the time the Psalms were written, this prayer makes use of a familiar, ordinary image.

Shepherds develop a close relationship with the sheep in their herd. They learn to distinguish not only between the bleating of various sheep but between the pain cries and the hunger cries of each sheep in the flock. Shepherds know their sheep not just as a mass, but as individuals. The statement "God is my shepherd" calls to mind all of these associations as attributes of God.

If God is like a shepherd, then the person praying is like a sheep. Over time, sheep come to know their shepherd. A shepherd can walk among her or his own sleeping flock, while a stranger's presence would cause pandemonium. Herds can mix at a watering hole and still be able to separate without confusion when the shepherds use their individual calls. Sheep know they can trust their shepherd.

What metaphor describes your feelings about the depths of life right now as you prepare to pray? What image evokes your understanding of the sacred? Look for a word picture that has some richness and depth to it.

I shall not be in want.

Many of us are more familiar with the common translation of this line as, "I shall not want," but this rendering has confused many through the ages. To today's reader, "I shall not want" sounds as though this prayer is telling us to give up our desires, our wants; a good person—a godly person—should have no wants of his or her own. The modern translation comes more to the point—because God is such a good shepherd, we will never go without. This is the theme that runs through the whole prayer and which is behind the choice of the shepherd metaphor; the psalmist knows that he can trust God and that, if he does so, all of his essential needs will be taken care of—he "shall not be in want."

What does the metaphor you've chosen assure you of?

He makes me lie down in green pastures, he leads me beside quiet waters, he restores my soul.

Green pastures? Quiet waters? This sounds like a paradise, especially in as arid a region as the Sinai. The previous assertion that "I will not be in want" seems justified if the shepherd can make good on such promises. These phrases are more than a description of a nice place to stop and rest. Green pastures mean that food is plentiful. Quiet waters mean that there is accessible fresh water in abundance. The third phrase—"he restores my soul"—means that body and spirit are taken care of. This continues to flesh out the metaphor—God is not only a shepherd but a good shepherd who can be trusted to take care of the flock.

Building on the image you've selected, how are you being cared for? What can you say about how the Sacred is treating you?

He guides me in paths of righteousness for his name's sake.

Some have read this as saying that God directs us on the "right" road for the sake of his reputation, his "name." However, in the first-century Jewish mind, a name is more than just a label; it's a description of a person's essence. A better reading, then, might be that God "guides me in paths of righteousness *because that's who he is.*" The psalmist is saying, "I know who you are, God. You're the kind of god who wants your children to succeed. You want us to do well and will lead us down the right road if we'll only follow."

Continue to explore the various dimensions of the metaphor with which you've decided to pray. What is true of this God simply because of who or what it is? What must this God do to be consistent with its own nature?

Even though I walk through the valley of the shadow of death

Although this phrase and the next really belong together, let's pause here to highlight something that is often overlooked, misunderstood, or misrepresented in discussions of the spiritual life: Living a faithful life, communing with the sacred, will not make everything easy. This point cannot be underscored enough. The realities of life and death, celebration and suffering, will still happen to you. There's no avoiding them. The "valley of the shadow of death" is real—pain, suffering, fear, and despair are all part of the real world and there is no way around them. Each and every one of us will walk through the valley more than once. Nothing, not even God, can make us happy for all of our days. The Buddha told of a way to end suffering, but said we would still feel grief and loss. Christianity may promise that through Christ we have overcome death, but there's still dying to contend with—as well as illness, old age, disappointment, frustration, and failure. The valley is part of life, and no one worth listening to ever said anything different.

Of what hard truths about life do you want to remind yourself? What still needs to be said?

I will fear no evil,
for you are with me; your rod and your staff, they comfort me.

What the Buddha did promise was that, while we can't escape grief and loss, we do not have to suffer. The psalmist tells us that while we do have to walk through "the valley of the shadow of death," we don't have to live in fear of it. We might say that this is the payoff of the regular practice of a spiritual discipline— not the elimination of hard times but rather the comforting knowledge that we are not alone on your journeys. The Unitarian Universalist minister Wayne Arnason writes, "Take courage friends. The way is often hard, the path is never clear, and the stakes are very high. Take courage. For deep down there is another truth: you are not alone."

The perspective of many who are engaged in regular spiritual practice is that we do not walk alone in either our sorrow or our joy, for we are always inextricably bound with all of life. We are, as Ralph Waldo Emerson puts it, "part and parcel of life" and that interconnectedness is, indeed, a "comfort."

Say something about the comfort and the confidence that you feel in the face of that reality because of what you know about the sacred.

You prepare a table before me in the presence of my enemies.

What a marvelous image! Again, note that the psalmist still has enemies and that, it would seem, they're still close at hand. In fact, he is among them, in their presence, at this very moment. This is not a "rose-colored glasses" prayer: The psalmist knows that he is threatened, surrounded by dangers. Imagine someone in a large corporation whom the rumor mill has falsely accused of some heinous faux pas. Everyone looks on him with suspicion and scorn. Then one day the C.E.O. comes into the lunchroom and announces that she has catered a lunch for one of her employees—a table is set with linens and fine china, carts of exquisite food are brought in, and the much maligned employee is invited to sit down while everyone else's jaw hangs open. This is more than vindication—it is redemption and restoration.

What would demonstrate to you your total victory over everything that troubles you? Can you think of as concrete an image as the psalmist does?

You anoint my head with oil, my cup overflows.

According to the books of 1 and 2 Samuel, anointing a King is the equivalent of crowning him. Priests and prophets were all anointed. It was also a common act of hospitality, a means of refreshing and reinvigorating the body. Some contemporary Arab communities still practice the custom of anointing visitors. The reference to anointing here is a symbol both of God honoring the psalmist and an act of comfort. Psalm 133 contains a reference to Moses anointing Aaron. The psalmist writes, "the precious ointment upon the head, that ran down upon the beard, even Aaron's beard: that went down to the skirts of his garments." Combined with the image of a cup overflowing, we are given the picture of God's grace being considerably more than enough—abundant, excessive, gratuitous generosity.

Can you think of a way of describing this feeling in your own words?

Surely goodness and mercy will follow me all the days of my life.
And I will dwell in the house of the Lord forever.

This conclusion could not be any further from the Twenty-Second Psalm's more forced optimism. That psalm encourages us to believe in God's generosity despite the lack of personal experience of grace and comfort. Here, the assurance is overflowing our cups and pouring down our faces and necks. It is on the banquet table before us. It is in the cool water and lush grasses. There can be no doubt at all.

How would you end this prayer?

If we now take the Twenty-Third Psalm, as we did the Lord's Prayer, and try to expose its framework, we see something like the following:

Begin with a metaphor for the holy.
Describe how the metaphor affects you.
Develop the metaphor further.
Recognize the reality that life will continue to be difficult.
Describe what gives you comfort.
Give voice to what reassures you.

Using this format, compose a prayer that reflects your situation and your understandings. For example,

O God, you are a playful puppy; I'll never be lonely. You knock me over in your desire to have fun. You return eagerly no matter how I behave. You calm my spirit. You remind me to keep things in perspective because the only thing that matters to you is love.

Even though life can threaten to crash in on me I will not be overcome; your bark and soft fur soothe me. You bring me to the park to play in the middle of the work week. You lick my face and my hands. We never get tired. Together we'll keep playing as long as we live. And the sun will shine always.

Thomas Merton's Prayer

My Lord God—I have no idea where I am going. I do not see the road ahead of me. I cannot know for certain where it will end. Nor do I even really know myself, and the fact that I think I am doing your will does not mean that I am actually doing so. But I believe that the desire to please you does, in fact, please you. And I hope that I have that desire in all I am doing. I hope that I will never do anything apart from that desire. And I know that if I do that, you will lead me by the right road though I may know nothing about it. Therefore, I will trust you always though I appear to be lost and in the shadow of death. I will not fear, for you are ever with me and will never leave me to face my perils alone.

THE TRAPPIST MONK Thomas Merton wrote this prayer and included it in his book *Thoughts in Solitude.* The popularity of this prayer shows that it strikes a chord with many people. I know of a minister who, when asked about it, said, "I know I shouldn't say this, but I think it's even better than the Lord's Prayer." Looking at this prayer's form step by step will help us understand how this Catholic monk's prayer can touch the hearts of so many Baptists, Episcopalians, Buddhists, and others who have spoken of its power.

My Lord God

The prayer begins with a statement about relationship. For Merton, God is understood as *Lord*. He could have said *Loving God*, or *Eternal Mystery*, or *Mother/Father God*. He chose, instead, to identify his God as his Lord in order to emphasize his understanding of God's sovereignty in his life; to declare that, in this encounter at least, he is relating to one who has full authority over him and to whom he is submissive. *Lord* is certainly a somewhat archaic term today. It carries with it a host of connotations. Rooting himself in his Catholic tradition, affirming aspects of this traditional understanding of the Divine, Merton communicates a lot with his first three words. Merton's choice need not be ours, just as this choice is not the one Merton makes in every prayer. Still, we can learn here, as we did when looking at the Lord's Prayer, to begin our prayers with an identification.

To whom, to what, do you pray?

I have no idea where I am going.
I do not see the road ahead of me.
I cannot know for certain where it will end.

There is a truth in these words that most of us can relate to, even if we wouldn't so readily relate it to others. None of us knows "where we're going"—not really. Even when we think we do we must one day face the inescapable reality that life is not entirely under our control. The unexpected, unaccounted for, uncontrolled, and uncontrollable happens with a regularity that should give the strongest of us pause. In our private moments, we do pause and wonder: What's going to happen to me? Do I really have what it takes to get through the things I'm facing? Will I be ready for what lies ahead?

Imagine that you are driving from New York to San Francisco on an unfamiliar route . . . without a map . . . in the fog . . . at night. At best you will be able to see the tiny portion of the road that is illuminated by your headlights. Beyond that is complete unknown territory, knowable only as you come to it. That's how we live our lives.

After clearly identifying the relationship that forms the context for this prayer, Merton describes his situation honestly—he, like so many of us, is confused and facing an uncertain future. There is no pretense here; this is a truly humble beginning. The foundational posture of this prayer is uncertainty. It is a prayer, not of strength, but of fundamental weakness.

What is your honest assessment of your place in the cosmos? Do you feel like the master of your destiny, the helpless pawn of fate, or something in between?

> *Nor do I even really know myself, and the fact that*
> *I think I am doing your will*
> *does not mean that I am actually doing so.*

Now, Merton takes things even a step further. Confession enters into this prayer, a wonderful demonstration of Knowing at its most unflinching. Merton knows that he does not know—not where his life is headed and not even everything in his own head and heart. He demonstrates his commitment not to pretend before his Lord; nothing but the unvarnished truth will be given voice in this prayer.

Most of us, on the other hand, expend a great deal of energy trying to look like we've got things pretty well together. We want to appear to have all the answers; we want to seem secure even if only within our own minds. If we're forced to recognize that the world is out of our control, we'll rally behind the conviction that we at least still have ourselves. We may not be master of our little worlds, but at least we can be master of what's going on within us.

Except that we're not. Most psychological theories teach that a great deal of our motivation for the way we are in the world is not only out of our control but beyond our comprehension. It operates below the level of our consciousness. We simply don't—can't—know why we do much of what we do. Religions have been teaching this for millennia. In this portion of the prayer, Merton honestly faces this reality of his life, which is the reality of all of our lives—even when we're doing what we think is right our actions may have effects and motivations of which we are unaware. In fact, at some level we may be doing the very thing we're trying not to do, and the hardest truth is that we just can't know for sure.

What is it that would be hard for you to admit yet which in your innermost silence you know to be true? What would be left if you stripped away all the posturing and pretensions and allowed yourself to stand naked in all your imperfections?

> *But I believe that the desire to please you does,*
> *in fact, please you.*

This is an important theological statement. Merton is asserting that although the God to whom he prays is sovereign and he himself is lost and confused, God does not demand more than we can give. This God may be Lord, yet this God is also loving and willing to overlook our many shortcomings and failures. We don't have to know where we're going; we don't even have to know what we're doing all the time. We simply have to try our best, and that will be enough.

Note that this is a faith statement. Merton does not say "I know," but "I believe." This is not something about which we can have incontrovertible, conclusive proof. At heart the sacred and the holy are Mystery, and as St. Augustine writes, the best we can do in the face of Mystery is talk in analogies. Yet this is enough for Merton. God does not demand perfection of us; he does not demand proof from God. His belief is enough to keep him moving.

What do you believe? Is that belief enough for you?

> *And I hope that I have that desire in all I am doing.*
> *I hope that I will never do anything apart from that desire.*

Merton now offers a response, an action on his part based on what he has said so far. He understands God to be his Lord. He knows that his life is out of his own control, as is his very being.

Yet he believes that his sovereign God is loving enough to overlook his failures and accept his best efforts. Merton states his desire to make a good effort. He declares his intention to try to live his life always doing his best to please God. Note the way he uses the qualifying phrase, "I hope," in each sentence. Even here, he acknowledges his weakness and capacity for failure. A prayer found in varying form in a number of mystic traditions is, "God, give me the desire to desire you." This is essentially what Merton is praying: "I hope that I have the desire to try my best. I promise to try to try."

What promise are you willing to make?

And I know that if I do that, you will lead me by the right road
though I may know nothing about it.

This is Merton's first expression of certainty—"I know that if I do that, you will lead me by the right road . . ." Until this moment he has spoken of hopes, desires, and his own fundamental uncertainty, yet in this promise he rests. Amidst all of his uncertainty, Merton now lands solidly on a truth of which he is certain. He knows that when he tries with true intention, God makes good use of his best efforts. He knows, because his own experience bears it out, that even the rocky roads he's traveled have taken him to good places even if he wasn't aware of where he was going at the time.

Merton doesn't claim that his faith in God will give him a new clarity of vision. He doesn't say that the road signs will become more obvious—"this way, right road; that way, wrong road." In fact, he as much as says that he expects to continue to be unable to discern the right road from the wrong. He doesn't imagine that he will be any more able to choose the right road, but he has renewed faith that God both can and will. In that certainty, he takes comfort and strength.

What do you know with certainty? On what do you rest secure?

Therefore, I will trust you always though I appear to be lost and in
the shadow of death.
I will not fear, for you are ever with me and will never leave me to
face my perils alone.

Merton's prayer begins with confusion and ends with conviction. He does not say that his fundamental condition has
changed—he is still lost and confused. His attitude toward this
condition, however, has changed dramatically. Now, rather than
focusing on what he doesn't know—where he's going—he
emphasizes what he does know: He will never be left alone. He
may still be uncertain, but he's no longer fearful. He trusts that
even when he feels most lost and in danger he is in safe hands.

People often imagine that if only they have enough, or the
right kind, of faith in some kind of divinity all of their problems
will vanish. All confusion, all concern will be replaced by joy and
peaceful bliss. Merton, however, knows that he will always have
times in his life when he finds himself "lost and in the shadow of
death." He knows that he will often wonder if he's doing the right
thing. He knows that he will face innumerable perils in his life,
even with his faith in God. His faith doesn't change any of that,
but it does change the way he faces these facts, for it gives him the
certainty that, in the words of Julian of Norwich, "All will be well,
all will be well, all manner of things will be well."

What confidence comes to you with this prayer? How have
you changed because of it?

One of things that makes this prayer so powerful, especially to
modern seekers, is that it is very logical. This prayer moves from
confession of ignorance and weakness to a profession of faith in
God's wisdom and strength.

After stripping this prayer to its fundamental essentials, the
following elements emerge:

Give a name to the relationship you have with the sacred
and holy.

Acknowledge the aspect of the human condition that currently concerns you.

Confess your own deepest weakness.

Make a statement of your belief about the sacred.

Offer a response, intention, or promise.

Remember how this has been shown to be true in your life.

Make a declaration of the confidence that comes from this recognition.

Using this format, compose a prayer that reflects your situation and your understandings. For example,

Nameless Presence—there is so much more that I don't know than what I do know. I could spend a lifetime studying one aspect of one facet of one thing and still only scratch the surface. And I don't even know all that I don't know—I often think I know things, and even more often pretend to know things, of which I am actually completely ignorant. Yet I believe that what I most need to know is my relationship, through you, to all that is. And I want to be satisfied with this. For I know that when I rest in this simple knowledge, all that I need comes to me. Therefore I will gently return my focus to you, who was and is and evermore shall be, and all will be well.

A Bodhisattva's Prayer

May I be a protector to those without protection,
a leader for those who journey,
and a boat, a bridge, a passage
for those desiring the further shore.
May the pain of every living creature
be completely cleared away.
May I be the doctor and the medicine
and may I be the nurse
for all sick beings in the world
until everyone is healed.
Just like space
and the great elements such as earth,
may I always support the life
of all the boundless creatures.
And until they pass away from pain
may I also be the source of life
for all the realms of varied beings
that reach unto the ends of space.

THIS CHANT/PRAYER WAS WRITTEN by the eighth-century Indian
monk Shantideva. The author of several texts, he is most well
known for his long poem, the *Bodhicaryavatara* ("A Guide to the
Bodhisattva Way of Life"). This prayer comes from a longer litany

of Bodhisattva vows in the third chapter.

A Bodhisattva is a tremendously important figure in Buddhist teaching. She or he is one who has almost attained Nirvana and complete freedom from the cycle of birth and death yet has chosen to remain in the realm of *samsara* (illusion) to help all other beings find their way. In some ways analogous to the angels of some religions and the demigods of others, Bodhisattvas nonetheless represent an ideal toward which many Buddhists strive. Shantideva addresses his poem to those who are on such a path. The *Bodhicaryavatara* is especially revered within the Tibetan Buddhist traditions, and the fourteenth Dalai Lama, Tenzin Gyatso, praises the power of its teaching.

The vast majority of Buddhists do not pray in a way familiar to most people from Judeo-Christian traditions. With only a few exceptions, Buddhists do not believe in a deity toward whom prayers can be directed. Buddhists do not generally petition, negotiate with, or placate a deity, and yet they do pray.

Buddhism does have a vibrant tradition of chant in which practitioners, alone or in groups, recite sacred texts that have been handed down to them, sometimes across thousands of years. Many of these chants, such as the well-known Prajnaparamita Heart Sutra, are distillations of longer discourses—Cliff's Notes, if you will, of complex Buddhist teachings. Some, as in this example, are intended to represent the practitioner's deepest desires.

May I be a protector to those without protection

This prayer does not begin with any kind of invocation. No one—no thing—is being addressed. Buddhism has often been understood as an atheistic religion, yet this is not entirely accurate. Many Buddhist texts make mention of gods and goddesses—sometimes hundreds and thousands of them and Bodhisattvas function in many ways as demigods. Buddhism is a descendent of Hinduism, and echoes of the Hindu pantheon can be found in Buddhism just as Christianity retains, even while it alters, Jewish scripture.

The historical Buddha, himself, was ambiguous on the subject of deity. When asked if gods and goddesses were real, the Buddha replied with the somewhat enigmatic, "That is a question which does not tend toward edification." In other words, whether or not there is a divinity is the wrong question. After all, if you are on a spiritual quest and there is a divinity you will try your best to live the best life you can, to do the most good you can, and to make the world a better place. And if you are on a spiritual quest and there is not a divinity, you will no doubt still try your best to live the best life you can, to do the most good you can, and to make the world a better place. The important question, then, is how to live such a life.

Such an attitude can be applied to prayer as well. If there is a God, that God will hear us. Yet even if there isn't, we can still give voice to our highest aspirations and that which is deepest within us.

May I be a protector to those without protection,
a leader for those who journey,
and a boat, a bridge, a passage
for those desiring the further shore.

A traditional Bodhisattva vow from the Zen tradition is:

Sentient beings are numberless; I vow to save them. Desires are inexhaustible; I vow to put an end to them. The Dharmas are boundless; I vow to master them. The Buddha-way is unattainable; I vow to attain it.

In short, the task is impossible; yet the speaker vows to accomplish it.

Shantideva's vows are no less extravagant. In this section, the practitioner expresses her or his intention to be whatever others have the most need for. This is one of the hallmarks of Bodhisattvas—they adapt themselves to the needs of others rather than the other way around. In fact, many say that the most annoying and obnoxious people in our lives are actually Bodhisattvas giving us the challenges we need to learn and to grow!

Whereas Thomas Merton acknowledges in his prayer that all

he can do is try, Shantideva vows a level of service that seems impossible. Is this masochism—setting the bar so high that no one could possibly attain it? Not exactly. Buddhists believe that the way we think shapes the reality we experience. If we think of ourselves as victims, we will continually experience ourselves as victimized. If we think of ourselves as survivors, we will again and again see ourselves survive. The recitation of a prayer such as Shantideva's continually reinforces our desire to achieve this level of generous compassion; the more we claim for ourselves such lofty aspirations, the less often we accept the more lowly ones. This kind of prayer not only gives voice to our deepest desires, it helps to shape them.

In some ways this prayer anticipates the classic Christian prayer attributed to St. Francis of Assisi—". . . where there is hatred, let me sow love; where there is injury, pardon; where there is doubt, faith . . ." Both are very powerful expressions of giving over one's own will, one's own agenda, for the greater good of others. Rather than going out into the world with a clear plan for how you are going to help everyone, you can just go out and meet people and see what they need. Unlike the stereotypical Christian missionary who wants to convert others to bring them to Christ, the Bodhisattva is willing to convert himself or herself into whatever is needed in order to help others find their way to Nirvana.

This is the specific focus of this first stanza—the phrase about "those desiring the further shore" is a reference to a fundamental Buddhist image for the quest for Nirvana. Life as we know it—life lived asleep, in delusion, *Samsara*—is imagined as one shore of a great ocean; the enlightened, free life, *Nirvana*, is the other shore. The spiritual journey, then, is the journey across this great ocean from the near shore to the further shore. Call it heaven, self-realization, perfection, enlightenment—this is the goal of the spiritual quest. In this part of the prayer, the practitioner declares her or his intention to do (and be) whatever is necessary to help other people reach this goal.

What do you see as the goal of the spiritual life, and what are some metaphors you might use to describe how you could help others to attain it?

May the pain of every living creature
be completely cleared away.
May I be the doctor and the medicine
and may I be the nurse
for all sick beings in the world
until everyone is healed.

The historical Buddha is said to have lived for forty years following his enlightenment, and during that time he taught continuously. Tradition holds that all of his teachings were remembered and eventually written down, so Buddhists have literally thousands of sacred texts to draw on. Still, all of it can be summed up in what is remembered as the Buddha's first teaching, the so-called Four Noble Truths:

Life is suffering.

Attachment is the cause of suffering.

One can learn to break free from attachment.

The "eight-fold path"—the so-called Middle Way, a life lived in the development of right understanding, right thought, right speech, right action, right livelihood, right effort, right mindfulness, and right concentration—is the way to break free.

The Sanskrit word that is translated as "suffering" is *dukkha*. This word can also mean impermanent, unsatisfying, transient. The Noble Truths teach that the reality that things are constantly changing is at the core of our existence. Since we want our lives to remain consistent, since we want something to hold on to, we experience this fundamental transience as suffering. This is the cause of all of our problems. This is the "illness" that infects us all. We want life to be something other than it is, and we suffer because of the dissonance.

Shakiyamuni Buddha is frequently referred to as *the Good Doctor*, and his teachings are often called *Medicine*. The second stanza draws on these metaphors to describe the human condition as essentially one of illness and the need for healing. How do you see our existential reality?

> *Just like space*
> *and the great elements such as earth,*
> *may I always support the life*
> *of all the boundless creatures.*

Here the practitioner allies herself or himself with nothing less than the limitlessness of space and the firm reality of dirt—nothing more vast and nothing more immediate. At first glance, it might appear that this prayer is all abstraction, yet here—between the farthest reaches of the cosmos and the ground beneath our feet—we see the guide by which all our specific actions can be measured: "May I always support the life of all the boundless creatures."

In other words, for Shantideva the question to continually ask one's self is, "Does this support life?" This is analogous to Mohandas Gandhi's famous question, How will my actions affect the poorest person in the world? or the measure used by the Iroquois Confederacy, How will this affect the seventh generation? "May I always support life" is a clear guideline—seemingly simple, but tremendously demanding.

What is your own bottom line, the standard by which you want to measure all of your actions, and to what do you ally yourself?

> *And until they pass away from pain*
> *may I also be the source of life*
> *for all the realms of varied beings*
> *that reach unto the ends of space.*

The scope of a Bodhisattva's concern is no small thing. In Buddhist cosmology, there are countless other realms, each with a myriad of worlds and innumerable beings. A Bodhisattva vows to support them all, even to the point of being their "source of life." In all ways, this is a prayer of self-giving, yet it has nothing of self-sacrifice about it, nothing of martyrdom. The Bodhisattva Kuan Yin ("She Who Hears the World's Cries") is said to have a thousand arms that reach out and do her good deeds effortlessly, as a person effortlessly reaches out to adjust a pillow while sleeping. A Bodhisattva is one who has taken into herself or himself these ideals so deeply that self and values become one and no sacrifice is needed to live those values. Since it is fundamental to Buddhist teaching that all things are interconnected, any good I do for you is also a good for me: There can be no sense of martyrdom in this ethical system.

Shantideva's fourth stanza reminds us of just how wide and deep the circle of our concern is. It is big enough to include not just you, your family, your acquaintances, and your country, not even just all humanity or even all the creatures on this planet, but rather every being everywhere, in every realm throughout all space. The Bodhisattva commits herself or himself to serving these myriad beings until each and every one has achieved enlightenment.

How far are you willing to go? To what level of service are you willing to commit yourself?

If we pare back this prayer to its core structure, the following elements emerge:

Metaphorically depict the spiritual journey and your intention to help others.
Metaphorically depict the essence of the human experience and how you can help.
Declare the boundaries of your alliance and the "bottom line" against which you will measure all of your actions.
Declare the boundaries of the circle of your concern.

Using this format, compose a prayer that reflects your situation and your understandings. For example,

May I be light to those in darkness,
food to the hungry,
and the alarm clock, the wake-up call, the morning cup of
    coffee
for those who would need awaken.

May the fear of every being
be completely assuaged.
May I be the engineer and the architect
and the demolition crew,
assisting all alienated and isolated beings
until all of the dividing walls are completely torn down.

Just like air
and the element of water,
may I always cleanse and clarify
revealing truth in its myriad forms.

And until the earth falls into the sun,
may I inspire and encourage
the complete unfolding of beauty's potential
in all things throughout space and time.

Starhawk's Prayer

Hail, Guardians of the Watchtowers of the East, Powers of Air! We invoke you and call you, Golden Eagle of the Dawn, Star-seeker, Whirlwind, Rising Sun, Come! By the air that is Her breath, send forth your light. Be here now!

Hail, Guardians of the Watchtowers of the South, Powers of Fire! We invoke you and call you, Red Lion of the noon heat, Flaming One! Summer's warmth, Spark of Life, Come! By the fire that is Her spirit, send forth your flame. Be here now!

Hail, Guardians of the Watchtowers of the West, Powers of Water! We invoke you and call you, Serpent of the watery abyss, Rainmaker, Gray-robed Twilight, Evening Star! By the waters of Her living womb, send forth your flow. Be here now!

Hail, Guardians of the Watchtowers of the North, Powers of Earth, Cornerstone of All Power. We invoke you and call you, Lady of the Outer Darkness, Black Bull of Midnight, North Star, Center of the whirling sky. Stone, Mountain, Fertile Field, Come! By the earth that is her body, send forth your strength. Be here now!

The circle is cast. We are between the worlds, beyond the bounds of time, where night and day, birth and death, joy and sorrow, meet as one. The fire is lit, the ritual is begun.

STARHAWK'S *The Spiral Dance* has been an introductory text for so many developing Wiccans that the Invocation she wrote for the chapter on "Creating Sacred Space" can serve us as a model.

One thing that Wicca and pagan religions of all sorts have in common is that there is no single sacred text or any founding figures. The neo-pagan movement is a modern interpretation of ancient earth-centered religions, particularly those originating in pre-Christian Europe. Due to extreme persecution under the rule of Christianity, little survives in direct descent from those pre-Christian traditions. Today, neo-pagan communities create their religious life and rites anew as they live them.

The creative nature of paganism keeps these traditions alive and lively, but it also means that there is nothing analogous to the Christian Lord's Prayer or the Jewish Twenty-Third Psalm for the Pagan. Some groups do keep and repeat rituals that have been handed down for generations, yet the vast majority create new rituals for each new occasion.

Perhaps more than any other religious community, Pagans understand their prayers to be efficacious; they believe that their prayers actually do something in the world. Pagans use the terms *magick* and *spells* to refer to prayers that accomplish something, that have an effect in the world. For a Pagan, it is most important to know the intention of a specific prayer and the proper form; the words used can flow spontaneously in the moment.

Neo-pagan prayers are earth-centered almost by definition. *Pagan* is a Latin word meaning "country dweller," and ancient Romans used it to refer to anyone who didn't adopt one of the three major monotheistic religions—Judaism, Christianity, or Islam. Most scholars agree that this is because those who lived in the country were slower to adopt the new religions than those who lived in the cities; country dwellers were more likely to live with deep connection to the earth and reverence for the old ways.

Pagan imagery tends to be that of the natural world. Generally speaking, a modern neo-pagan invocation will call upon the four directions of east, south, west, and north, and the four elements of air, water, fire, and earth. Sometimes two more directions are honored—above and below; sometimes the element of spirit is invoked in addition to the others. It is not unusual for some of the animals, birds, colors, emotions, and activities that are associated with the various directions to be named as well.

Where does one find these associations? Whole shelves of your library or New Age bookstore are filled with books on Pagan symbolism, and the different traditions each have their own variations—dialects, if you will, of the commonly accepted lexicon of imagery. People interested in this kind of prayer are encouraged to explore the resources listed in the bibliography for more specific information. This exploration of Starhawk's prayer will use images and associations that are generally agreed upon in the neo-pagan community. You, of course, are free to come up with your own.

Hail, Guardians of the Watchtowers of the East, Powers of Air!
We invoke you and call you, Golden Eagle of the Dawn, Star-seeker,
Whirlwind, Rising Sun, Come! By the air that is Her breath, send
forth your light. Be here now!

Because the sun appears to rise in the east, the east is said to be the direction of the dawn. This makes it, by extension, the direction of spring time and new beginnings. It is also understood as home to the powers of the element of air. It is connected to the mind, to knowing and thinking.

What sounds, smells, colors, and animals would help you conjure up "the east" in your mind? What do you associate with "air?" Be as concrete or as poetic as you wish. Also ask yourself what is being born in your life at this time? Feel free to be flowery or direct, but have fun. Be dramatic.

Hail, Guardians of the Watchtowers of the South, Powers of Fire! We
invoke you and call you, Red Lion of the noon heat, Flaming One!
Summer's warmth, Spark of Life, Come! By the fire that is Her spirit,
send forth your flame. Be here now!

If the east is the direction of the dawn, then going around the compass clockwise makes the south the direction of noon time and summer. Not surprisingly, the south is also the home of the powers of fire. It is connected to our ambition, passion, and will. As with the east, think of imagery that paints a picture for you of these things. Remember that, as with all prayer, it is your own authentic connection to the words you say that truly matters. So, for instance, you may find the idea of "the south" to be one of dynamic energy or sweltering lethargy. "Fire" may conjure a candle or a conflagration in your mind. There is no single "correct" way to relate to these symbols.

Look at the world around you. What symbolizes "south" and "fire" for you? If you wish, look at your own life. Where do you have or need some of that power?

Hail, Guardians of the Watchtowers of the West, Powers of Water!
We invoke you and call you, Serpent of the watery abyss, Rainmaker,
Gray-robed Twilight, Evening Star! By the waters of Her living womb,
send forth your flow. Be here now!

Continuing around the circle of the seasons we come to the west, which is traditionally associated with dusk and autumn. It is the realm of the powers of water and, perhaps because of their fluidity, of emotion. We can also look at these directions as depicting the human life cycle—east is birth and childhood, south is adolescence and young adulthood, north is old age, and the west is the place of adulthood, of maturity.

From the crisp crunch of autumn leaves to the rushing flood of Niagara Falls, what symbolizes "west" to you? What emotions are you working with right now?

Hail, Guardians of the Watchtowers of the North, Powers of Earth,
Cornerstone of All Power. We invoke you and call you, Lady of the
Outer Darkness, Black Bull of Midnight, North Star, Center of the
whirling sky. Stone, Mountain, Fertile Field, Come! By the earth that
is her body, send forth your strength. Be here now!

Finally we arrive at the north, the place of midnight and the dark of winter; these associations make it natural to connect the north with deep mystery. It is also home to the element of earth. Since the North Star appears to be a center point around which the night sky revolves, and since earth literally and figuratively grounds us, the north is the direction of centering and inward grounding. You might imagine pitch-black midnight and frigid mid-winter as negative things, but the majority of neo-pagan traditions see nature through a positive lens. Fire may be destructive, yet that destruction is also transformative; true darkness may be frightening, yet it can also calm and comfort.

What can you say about the dark of night? What comes to you from the north?

The circle is cast. We are between the worlds, beyond the bounds of time, where night and day, birth and death, joy and sorrow, meet as one. The fire is lit, the ritual is begun.

Most neo-pagan invocations include some kind of summary stanza. Here, the intent of the prayer is made explicit—a circle has been carved out of the everyday world to create a sacred space "between the worlds." It should be noted that this prayer is only part of a larger Wiccan ritual. The energies just collected need to be directed toward some end, and the circle just cast need to be "opened." Think of it as inviting friends over—you'd want to do something with them before sending them home.

What is your intention for praying this prayer? What kind of space are you creating?

The structure of neo-Pagan prayers is relatively easy to see. Perhaps this is because they have not yet been enshrined as sacred in and of themselves; their usefulness is still considered of paramount importance. Also, in most of the Pagan traditions, creative improvisation is still highly valued. A clear pattern helps improvised prayers to be recognizable as invocations. Think of classic blues music. Nearly all traditional blues tunes are built on the same progression of chords, instantly recognizable beneath the various melodies played above them. Yet despite this formulaic similarity, musicians have created a huge repertoire of songs that are all unique and distinct. The same is true of a Wiccan invocation. Its form might be instantly recognizable, but the specifics are as unique as the individual who is praying.

The limits of this prayer form are the limits of your imagination. Each time you cast a circle you may well use a completely different set of images depending on your mood and the nature of your intention. On the other hand, some of these figures may become old friends whom you call on again and again.

If we take Starhawk's invocation and strip it of all but its core structure, the following elements emerge:

Begin by calling on the images you associate with the east.
Call on that which you associate with the south.
Call on the symbols you connect with the west.
Call on the things that make you think of the north.
Describe your intention and the sacred space you have created through your prayer.

Using this format, compose a prayer that reflects your situation and your understandings. For example,

Spirits of the East, Powers of Air, I greet you! I call upon the soft dew of the dawn, the fragrant breezes of springtime, the gentle coo of the morning dove—watch over that which is coming to birth in my life, all that is almost but not yet. By the air that surrounds the whole earth and flows within me, come softly.

Spirits of the South, Powers of Fire, I greet you! I call upon the strong sun of the noonday, the dynamic heat of the summer's burning, the invincible roar of the lion—lend me strength whenever I fear and falter. By the fire that transforms and enlightens, come brightly.

Spirits of the West, Powers of Water, I greet you! I call upon the quiet cool of the evening, the crisp colors of autumn, the dignified grace of the dolphin—help me to swim through the ebbs and flows of life, maintaining equilibrium and equanimity. By the water that buoys, come steadily.

Spirits of the North, Powers of Earth, I greet you! I call upon the impenetrable silence of midnight, the clarifying cold of midwinter, the unyielding stability of the mountains—ground my every step and support my every endeavor. By the earth that makes all things grow, come decisively.

The circle is cast. I stand at the balance point where within and without, above and below, sacred and secular unite and intertwine. The dance has begun. So shall it be.

SIMPLY PRAY

Where shall I look when I praise You? Upward or
downward, inward or outward? For You are the
place in which all things are contained: there is
no other place beside You: all things are in You.

—Hermes

In Genesis 28 Jacob stops while travelling at what the text calls "a certain place." Apparently there's nothing particularly remarkable about it—he doesn't stop here because it's an especially well-known place, or because it's considered a tremendously holy place, or even because it's an exceptionally pretty place to bed down for the night. We're told that he stops here because the sun has gone down. It's simply too dark to continue.

Yet here, in this unnamed "certain place," Jacob has a dream in which he sees a stairway (or in some translations a ladder) connecting heaven and earth with angels going up and down on it, and he hears the voice of God making promises that would take our breath away. When Jacob wakes up from his dream he utters the memorable words, "Surely the Lord is in this place and I did not know it . . . this is none other than the house of God . . . the gate of heaven." From the stone he's been using as his pillow, he makes an altar.

What happened to Moses with the burning bush happens here with Jacob. This "certain place" is nothing special, yet with a jolt, Jacob realizes that God is in this very place.

We can understand this story as a story about the religious evolution from worship of local deities to the recognition that God transcends place. Yet there's something else going on here, something deeper. Jacob seems to miss this deeper point. We often do, too. When Jacob recognizes that God is with him in this "certain place" he immediately begins to think of it differently. The convenient place to stop for the night becomes a Holy Place—"the house of God"—and he erects an altar there to make sure no one mistakes it for an ordinary place. In so doing, though, he inadvertently binds God to place once again, only now it's this new place instead of the old place his ancestors knew. God, now, is in *this* place. And if, a little further along on the journey, someone asks him where to find God, he will say, "Back there at that stone altar along the side of the road. That's where you'll find God."

That's what we often do, too. Too often. We encounter the sacred somewhere and declare that place to be the holy of holies where the sacred can be found. We erect little altars and light sacred incense and return to it over and over and over again. This book, this building, this behavior—that's where you'll find it. But the divine shows up in unexpected places, places the divine was never before thought to be. We all get caught up in looking *there*, where our last encounter took place, and forget to look anywhere else, least of all *here*, the new place where God is.

The lesson of Jacob's experience is that "God is in *all* places." In fact, the mystery that transcends all naming and knowing, the depth we are looking for, is in us. In the Christian scriptures, Jesus speaks of being in God and God being in him and our being in them; the Apostle Paul speaks of Christ being within each of us. In Zen Buddhism, Buddha Nature is not just within each person but is the essential nature of each and every person and all of the "ten thousand things" that make up reality. The Hebrew Scriptures offer us the beautifully evocative lesson that "God is as close as our breath," a thought echoed in Islam's Qur'an, which says that God is "as close as the throbbing vein in our neck." The holy is not "out there," in this place or that place; the holy is in here, as close as the air in our lungs and the blood in our veins.

A Hassidic story tells of an old widow named Rachel who lives in a small hut on the outskirts of a small village on the edge of a tiny Eastern European country. She is poor—very, very poor—but she lives life as best she can. One night she has a dream in which a voice tells her to travel to the capital city, to go to the bridge that leads to the palace, and to look under the bridge, where she will find a treasure. Awaking the next morning Rachel thinks to herself, "what an odd dream," and goes on about her day.

That night, though, Rachel has the dream again. Again the voice, again the journey, again the discovery of treasure. "How strange!" she says to herself the next morning, but doesn't think much more about it.

Yet when she has the exact same dream for the third night in a row—the same voice telling her to take the same journey to the capital to look under the same bridge with the same fantastic result—she decides that she has to do something about it. "After all," she says to herself, "a dream you have three nights in a row you ought to listen to."

So Rachel closes up her home and sets off. It is a very long journey to the capital. She travels through forests and over hills. Sometimes she manages to catch a ride on a passing cart, but mostly she walks. Finally, after many days, she arrives at the capital city.

Very quickly, she makes her way to the bridge that leads to the palace, but almost as quickly she discovers that she has a problem. The bridge is guarded by armed guards twenty-four hours a day and she can think of no way of getting beneath the bridge undetected. Rachel sits down by the side of the road and tries to think of what to do next.

Rachel sits there for so long that she attracts the attention of the captain of the guards, who comes over to see what this odd old woman is doing. "Old woman," he asks, "what are you doing sitting here for so long?" Well, Rachel is an honest woman, so she tells the young captain about her dreams. The captain begins to laugh. "Don't be such a fool. Dreams can't tell you anything. Why, if I'd listened to my dreams I'd have long ago left my comfortable home here in the capital and made a long and arduous journey to a tiny village on the outskirts of our country. And there, in a tiny hut on the outskirts of the village I'd have found a widow named Rachel and, digging beneath her hearthstone, I'd have found a treasure. Old woman, don't bother listening to your dreams."

"Thank you for your story and your advice," Rachel says, and she immediately begins her journey back to her home. She travels through forests and over hills. Sometimes she manages to catch a ride on a passing cart, but mostly she walks. Finally, after many days, she arrives in her village. Immediately she goes to her home and digs beneath the hearthstone, and there she finds more gold than she has ever even imagined.

Rachel does two things with this gold. First, she takes a portion and sends it to the captain of the guards with a note that reads, "Young man, listen to your dreams." With the rest she builds a temple, and high above the entrance she places a plaque that reads, "Sometimes you have to travel far to discover what is near."

So often we imagine that life's depths are out there—or in there—somewhere far away, and that the distance is immeasurable. Yet life is not out there; that's only where we've erected the altars. Life is right here—as close as our breathing, as close as the pulsing vein in our necks, as close as our dreaming.

Sometimes we imagine that we must either use the terms and conditions others have set down—the names and understandings of tradition or scripture—or we must reject the whole idea of a spiritual life. Yet those names and understandings were all once just the best attempts of people to express the experiences they had had, and were never really intended as barriers to our doing the same thing. As the Transylvanian Catholic, turned Lutheran, turned Calvinist, turned Unitarian preacher Dávid Ferenc put it in 1568, "Faith is a gift of God." And who can argue with the gift God has decided to give to you? Your faith is between you and its source.

This study of prayer is intended as a tool to help you dig beneath your own hearthstone to discover the treasures awaiting you. It is intended to help you bypass the concepts and creeds until you have experiences for yourself that might give them meaning. So pick up your beads. Open your eyes. Open your ears. Open your heart. And know that God—or whatever it is that you decide to call that toward which the name *God* is intended to point—is in this very place.

Resources for Your Search

Scriptures

Borg, Marcus, ed. *Jesus and Buddha: The Parallel Sayings.* Berkeley, CA: Ulysses Press, 1997. While not, strictly speaking, a scripture, this book is included here as it brings together the words of the founders of two of the great religions—Buddhism and Christianity—setting side by side their teachings on such themes as "Compassion," "Materialism," and "The Inner Life."

Duchesne-Guillemin, Jacques, trans. *The Hymns of Zarathustra: A translation of the Gāthās together with introduction and commentary.* Boston: Beacon Press, 1952. Not generally included on the top ten list of familiar scriptures, this ancient text gives the insights of Zarathustra, also known as Zoroastra, whose teaching—Zoroastrianism—influenced Greek philosophy and can be seen in Judaism and Christianity as well.

Elliott, Neil and Geshe Kelsang Gyatso, trans. *Guide to the Bodhisattva's Way of Life: A Buddhist Poem for Today.* Cumbria, England: Tharpa Publications, 2002. This is a very accessible translation of the long-poem scripture of the eight-century Indian monk Shantideva. This text is said to be a favorite of the Dalai Lama.

Khan, Muhammad Zafrulla, trans. *The Qur'an: Arabic text with a new translation.* New York: Olive Branch Press, 1997. There are obviously many translations of Islam's holy book. This translation "aims to make the study of the Qur'an broadly accessible to as wide an English-speaking audience as possible." The translator was once foreign minister of Pakistan, president of the Seventeenth Session of the United Nations General Assembly, and both judge and president of the International Court of Justice at the Hague.

Lau, D. C., trans. *The Analects of Confucius.* London: Penguin Books, 1979. Shortly after his death in 497 B.C., Confucius' disciples collected his sayings in twenty books, which together make up the Analects. This particular edition includes an introduction and appendices that help place these teachings in their rightful context.

Mascaró, Juan, trans. *The Dhammapada.* London: Penguin Books, 1973. This translation of the Buddha's pithy teachings is, indeed, a classic. Most likely compiled in the third century B.C.E., the Dhammapada is a collection of short aphorisms that clearly address the major themes expounded at greater length in the thousands of Buddhists scriptures that followed.

Mitchell, Stephen, trans. *Tao te Ching: A new English version.* New York: Harper & Row, 1988. This seemingly slight scripture from the Taoist tradition is as packed with provocative wisdom as any text twenty times its size. Stephen Mitchell's translation, while not as academically accurate as some, resonates with the heart of deep insight.

The New Oxford Annotated Bible with the Apocrypha, Revised Standard Version. New York: Oxford University Press, 1977. There are, of course, many translations of the Bible, but the RSV is considered one of the most accurate, and the annotations make this a dream for studying.

Wilson, Andrew, ed. *World Scripture: A Comparative Anthology of Sacred Texts*. St. Paul, MN: Paragon House, 1995. This project of the International Religious Foundation brings together passages from the scriptures of Buddhism, Christianity, Confucianism, Hinduism, Islam, Jainism, Judaism, Shinto, Sikhism, Taoism, and Zoroastrianism, as well as prayers and proverbs from a number of other traditions. The quotations are organized around general themes and demonstrate the differences and commonalities to humanity's search for answers.

Other Texts

Alexander, Scott, ed. *Everyday Spiritual Practice: Simple Pathways for Enriching Your Life*. Boston: Skinner House Books, 2001. An anthology of writings by nearly forty Unitarian Universalist clergy and laity describing the varied spiritual practices that they, themselves, use to "tend the garden of their souls"—from reading scripture to running, from family time to fasting.

Barry, William A. *Paying Attention to God: Discernment in Prayer*. Notre Dame, IN: Ave Maria Press, 1990. Barry, a Catholic priest, writes, "I am convinced that we encounter God in a mysterious way and that God wants a personal relationship with each of us." This book is an exploration of those convictions.

Bloom, Anthony. *Beginning to Pray*. Mahwah, NJ: Paulist Press, 1970. This eloquent book evocatively explores the idea of prayer as the way to develop a relationship with God. Bloom writes with the gentle yet assured voice of one who knows whereof he speaks. The book itself is a spiritual encounter.

—————————. *Living Prayer*. Springfield, IL: Templegate Publishers, 1966. Here Bloom looks at the essence of prayer, specific prayers such as the Lord's Prayer and the Jesus Prayer, and even such problems as unanswered prayers and how to deal with our false images of God and of ourselves.

Budapest, Zsuzsanna E. *Grandmother of Time*. San Francisco: HarperSanFrancisco, 1989. One of the classics of the neo-pagan movement, this is "a sourcebook of rituals, spells, and holy days for those who revere the Goddess. It is intended to teach both beginners and experienced practitioners how to integrate this spirituality into their everyday lives."

Buechner, Frederick. *Faces of Jesus*. San Francisco: Harper & Row, 1974. This book is a beautiful meditation in words and pictures on the many ways Jesus has been depicted throughout the centuries. Buechner's prose is as lovely as the paintings.

Daido Loori, John, ed. *Zen Mountain Monastery Liturgy Manual*. Mt. Tremper, NY: Dharma Communications, 1998. This is the collection of chants and texts used by the students and monastic community of Zen Mountain Monastery, a traditional Zen monastery in upstate New York.

DelBene, Ron. *The Breath of Life: a Simple Way to Pray*. Nashville, TN: Upper Room Books, 1992. The first of three books in the "Breath of Life Series," this one explores and explains the powerful practice of "breath prayer." (The other two are The Hunger of the Heart and Alone with God.)

de Mello, Anthony. *Sadhana: Christian Exercises in Eastern Form*. Liguori, MO: Ligouri/Triumph, 1978. This Catholic monk who was raised in India offers one hundred imaginative prayer exercises in a veritable (and venerable) "how to" book for this approach to prayer.

Edmonson, Robert, trans. *The Practice of the Presence of God*. Brewster, MA: Paraclete Press, 1985. This little book by the sixteenth-century monk Brother Lawrence consists of four "conversations" and fifteen letters expanding on the author's humble practice of living in the presence of God. This Christian Classics edition also includes a selection of "Spiritual Maxims" and more biographical information.

The teachings of this gentle monk are simple yet far from simplistic, and his work offers a vivid portrait of one who took the idea of a relationship with Christ and made it a reality in his life.

Edwards, Tilden. *Living in the Presence: Spiritual Exercises to Open Our Lives to the Awareness of God.* New York: HarperCollins, 1987. Edwards, one of the founders of the Shalem Institute for Spiritual Formation, provides readers with a gentle and practical guide to living a life of spiritual awareness in our day and age.

Fox, Matthew. *Meditations with Meister Eckhart.* Santa Fe, NM: Bear & Company, 1983. Eckhart was a Christian mystic of the thirteenth century who was branded a heretic in his own day and is now embraced as a teacher of great insight. These passages can be the source of endless meditation.

—————————. *One River, Many Wells.* New York: Jeremy P. Tarcher/Putnam, 2000. This book shows how the tenants of "creation spirituality" and "deep ecumenism" can be found throughout the world's religious traditions. It includes eighteen "new myths and visions" that might guide religious seekers in the twenty-first century.

—————————. *Original Blessing: A Primer in Creation Spirituality.* New York: Jeremy P. Tarcher/Putnam, 1983. This seminal work by the visionary (and controversial) Matthew Fox introduced the world to a Western spirituality that focuses on God's "original blessing" rather than humanity's so-called "original sin."

Hall, Thelma. *Too Deep for Words: Rediscovering Lectio Divina.* New York: Paulist Press, 1988. A modern introduction to the ancient Christian practice of lectio divina. Hall ends the book with over five hundred scriptural texts, divided into fifty themes, to use in prayer.

Henry, Gray and Susannah Marriott. *Beads of Faith: Pathways to Meditation and Spirituality Using Rosaries, Prayer Beads, and Sacred Words.* London: Carroll & Brown, 2002. A beautifully illustrated book, *Beads of Faith* provides a look at prayer bead rituals from around the world and gives the flavor of these practices.

Johnson, Willard. *Riding the Ox Home: A History of Meditation from Shamanism to Science.* Boston: Beacon Press, 1986. Bringing together such disparate figures as the Buddha, Socrates, Henry David Thoreau, and the American psychic Edgar Cayce, Johnson creates a wide-ranging study of mysticism across time and cultures. But this is not just another scholarly survey; its ultimate goal is to show "how meditation can help to heal psychic wounds and lead to authentic self-understanding and self-fulfillment."

Katz, Steven, ed. *Mysticism and Religious Traditions.* Oxford, England: Oxford University Press, 1983. The ten essays here "discuss the contexts of mysticism and the social mediation of mystical experience within all of the world's major religions." Definitely leaning toward the academic, but fascinating nonetheless.

Keating, Thomas. *Foundations for Centering Prayer and the Christian Contemplative Life.* New York: Continuum International Publishing Group, 2002. This one volume contains three of Father Keating's most important books. In *Open Mind, Open Heart,* he introduces the practice of centering prayer. In *Invitation to Love,* he looks at the theological and psychological underpinnings of this practice. Finally, in *The Mystery of Christ,* he develops a scriptural and theological grounding for centering prayer. Together, these books build a strong foundation for this modern way of prayer.

Ladinsky, Daniel. *The Gift: Poems by Hafiz the Great Sufi Master.* New York: Penguin Books, 1999. Ladinsky has made a career of translating the poems of Shams-ud-din Muhammad Hafiz, the fourteenth-century Sufi sage and poet. This is his most complete collection, but *The Subject Tonight Is Love* and *I Heard God Laughing* are also recommended.

LeShan, Lawrence. *How to Meditate: A Guide to Self-Discovery.* Boston: Bantam Books, 1975. A classic in the field, this is one of the first books to seek to articulate a "core teaching" of meditative technique, removed from the cultural conditioning of any specific religious tradition.

Loder, Ted. *Guerrillas of Grace: Prayers for the Battle.* Philadelphia: Innisfree Press, 1984. Loder is a United Methodist pastor and a poet of prayer. This collection offers an example of what modern prayers can sound like.

Mascetti, Manuela Cunn and Priya Hemenway. *Prayer Beads.* New York: Viking Compass, 2001. Sold in a gift box including a set of sandalwood mala, this lovely little book is a fine introduction to the use of prayer beads.

Merton, Thomas. *Contemplative Prayer.* New York: Doubleday Books, 1971. This is a brief but profound look at contemplative prayer by the Trappist monk who defined spirituality for a generation.

—————————. *Mystics and Zen Masters.* New York: Farrar, Straus and Giroux, 1961. Long before the idea of Buddhist-Christian dialog became common, this Trappist monk found deep commonalities between the contemplative spirituality of his tradition and that practiced by Buddhist monks.

—————————. *Thoughts in Solitude.* New York: Farrar, Straus and Giroux, 1956. This is Merton's look at the contemplative path from the inside. Brief, but moving.

Morgan, Henry, ed. *Approaches to Prayer: A Resource Book for Groups and Individuals.* Harrisburg, PA: Morehouse

Publishing, 1991. Briefly skimming this book will forever dispel the notion that there is only one way to pray. Actually reading it from cover to cover will give a deep appreciation of prayer as a playful activity and greatly increase your repertoire of approaches to prayer.

Mottola, Anthony, trans. *The Spiritual Exercises of St. Ignatius.* New York: Doubleday, 1964. This is one of the classics of Christian theology. Composed in 1533, it has influenced countless saints and seekers, and its systematic approach to prayer is the backbone of Ignatian retreats to this day.

Nhat Hanh, Thich. *The Miracle of Mindfulness: A Manual on Meditation.* Boston: Beacon Press, 1987. This Vietnamese poet, Buddhist monk, and peace activist has become one of the major communicators of Buddhism to the West. This book is a clear and concise guide to a number of different meditation practices.

——————————. *Present Moment Wonderful Moment: Mindfulness Verses for Daily Living.* Berkeley, CA: Parallax Press, 1990. This collection of English translations (with commentary) of the gathas used in Nhat Hanh's Vietnamese Buddhist tradition demonstrates the way one can make the most ordinary of daily activities into opportunities for mindfulness and provides an excellent introduction to gatha practice.

——————————. *The Plumb Village Chanting Book.* Berkeley, CA: Parallax Press, 1991. This book contains the chants, prayers, and gathas used by Thich Nhat Hanh's order.

——————————. *A Guide to Walking Meditation.* New York: Fellowship Publications, 1985. Just what the title says—an introduction to the practice of "walking meditation," an exercise in bringing the stillness one finds on a meditation cushion into the activity of the day.

Nouwen, Henri. *The Way of the Heart.* New York: Ballentine Books, 1981. This Dutch Catholic priest has a way of describing the spiritual path that speaks to a generation of seekers. This small book is a profound meditation on solitude, silence, and prayer.

Peers, E. Allison, trans. *Dark Night of the Soul.* New York: Doubleday Books, 1959. The phrase "dark night of the soul" has become a bit of pop spirituality jargon, but the one who coined the term, the Spanish mystic St. John of the Cross, is far more subtle and nuanced than one might imagine.

——————————. *Interior Castle.* New York: Doubleday Books, 1961. This classic of contemplative spirituality by the Christian saint Teresa of Avila is one of the most poetic depictions of the spiritual quest.

Postema, Don. *Space for God: The Study and Practice of Prayer and Spirituality.* Grand Rapids, MI: CRC Publications, 1983. Don Postema combines his own insights on the spiritual quest with quotations from a variety of traditions and the artwork of Vincent Van Gogh to create an eight-week course on prayer. Individuals can benefit from working through his eight chapters, and this program makes an ideal group study.

Richardson, Peter Tufts. *Four Spiritualities: Expressions of Self, Expressions of Spirit.* Palo Alto, CA: Davies-Black Publishing, 1996. In a very readable book, Richardson brings together insights from diverse spiritual traditions and modern psychology to explore the four primary spiritual paths, offering the reader the opportunity to discover for himself or herself an authentic spirituality.

Smith, Martin L. *The Word Is Very Near You: A Guide to Praying with Scripture.* Cambridge, MA: Cowley Publications, 1989. Like Thelma Hall's book, this is a very readable introduction to the history and modern expression of lectio divina. Smith also includes scripture for meditation, grouped into thirty themes.

—————————. *Reconciliation: Preparing for Confession in the Episcopal Church.* Cambridge, MA: Cowley Publications, 1985. This might seem to be a resource with quite limited usefulness, but Smith's exploration of the meanings and methods of Confession is well worth reading even for non-Episcopalians. Among other things, he helps explain why the church's change of emphasis from "confession" to "reconciliation" is more than merely semantic. He also helps readers to see confession as far more than a route recitation of "bad deeds."

Starhawk. *The Spiral Dance: A Rebirth of the Ancient Religion of the Great Goddess.* San Francisco: Harper & Row, 1979. This is one of the most well-known and well-respected introductions to the theory and practice of modern Wicca.

Underhill, Evelyn. *Practical Mysticism: A Little Book for Normal People.* Surrey, England: Eagle, 1991. Originally published in 1914, this classic is one of the first books to attempt to demystify the subject of mysticism and recommend if "normal people."

Washington, James Melvin, ed. *Conversations with God: Two Centuries of Prayers by African Americans.* New York: HarperPerennial, 1995. This collection—stretching from the 1700s through the 1990s—demonstrates the power and the poignancy of voices that have too often been silenced.

Wiley, Eleanor. *A String and a Prayer: How to Make and Use Prayer Beads.* Boston: Red Wheel, 2002. Wiley's book stands out for the section on how to create your own bead practice—whether for the start of a new day, to memorialize a life, to celebrate a marriage, or to honor religious or political leaders.

Wolters, Clifton, trans. *The Cloud of Unknowing and Other Works.* London: Penguin Books, 1961. This anonymous work from the late fourteenth century is a classic in Christian spirituality. The author's central theme is that the divine cannot be apprehended by the intellect; anyone who tries to understand God will find himself or herself enshrouded in a "cloud of unknowing," which can only be pierced by love.

Web Sites

Contemplative Outreach
(www.centeringprayer.com/frntpage.htm)
Dedicated to the work of Fathers Thomas Keating and Basil Pennington, among others, this site is dedicated to the practice and insights of Centering Prayer, a modern interpretation of ancient Christian contemplative prayer practices.

The Empty Bell
(www.emptybell.org/home.html)
This site is "a sanctuary for the study and practice of Christian meditation and prayer . . . . [giving] special attention to the Christian-Buddhist dialogue, to artistic expression of spiritual insight, and to the relationship between spirituality and stewardship of our bio-diverse natural world."

Holy Counting Beads
(www.thebeadsite.com/BBRS-01.html)
This is a branch from the TheBeadSite.com site, a site for The Center for Bead Research. This page provides information on Buddhist, Hindu, Catholic, Orthodox, Muslim, and Bah'ai use of beads, as well as links to a wealth of bead-related information.

Mysticism in the World's Religions
(www.digiserve.com/mystic/)
This site offers an interrelated collection of quotations from the great traditions of Buddhism, Christianity, Hinduism, Islam, Judaism, and Taoism. It can be searched by author, tradition, or cross-culturally by theme.

Peace Prayer
> (www.peaceprayer.org/index.html)
> A site dedicated specifically to prayers for peace from a variety of religious traditions. A very moving site.

Readings and Sites for the Spiritual Journey
> (www2.bc.edu/~anderso/sr/sr.html)
> A compendium of online resources for the spiritual seeker.

The Rosary Shop
> (www.rosaryshop.com/resources.php/request/flexWire)
> An online demonstration of how to use flex wire to make your own rosary. The techniques could be used, of course, for any style of prayer beads.

Sacred Space
> (www.jesuit.ie/prayer/)
> This site run by Irish Jesuits gently guides you through the practice of lectio devina. Thousands of people make this site a regular part of their daily routines.

The Shalem Institute for Spiritual Formation
> (www.shalem.org/index.html)
> This non-denominational organization offers a variety of experiential training programs in the contemplative tradition.

SpiritWalk
> (www.geocities.com/~spiritwalk/peaceprayers.htm)
> Another collection of peace prayers from a variety of the world's religions.

The World Community for Christian Meditation
> (www.wccm.org/frame849654.html)
> A worldwide community that follows the teaching of John Main, a Benedictine monk who reintroduced a Christian meditation practice based on the use of a mantra.

World Prayers
(www.worldprayers.org)
A multicultural collection of prayers categorized as Adoration, Celebration, Invocation, and Meditation. A unique feature is the "prayer wheel" that you can spin to randomly select a prayer.

Acknowledgments

I have always been fascinated by prayer. My family tells me that when I was a very little boy I would go outside after a rainstorm and pray for the worms that were drying up on the sidewalk. I have no memory of this, but it doesn't surprise me overly much. Whether the prayers of the Presbyterian and Methodist churches in which I was raised, the Transcendental Meditation practices I was taught as a child, the shamanic practices of the Yaqui brujo Don Juan Mateo that I encountered in my teens, or the activities of the Wiccan circles I discovered in my young adulthood, I have always hungered for direct encounter with the transcendent and have been both amazed and delighted by the variety of methods we humans have created to attain it. This book is my attempt to contribute to this rich tapestry, or to use another metaphor, to put another stone into the mosaic.

I am grateful, first and foremost, to that Living Spirit—which I call "God" yet which has myriad names—that reaches out to us and inspires us to reach back.

I am thankful to the people at the Shalem Institute for Spiritual Formation—both the teachers and the students—who helped me realize that it is not we who pray but God who prays in us. Our job is to get out of the way and learn to listen to God's prayer.

I want to thank all those at, especially, the First Universalist Church of Yarmouth (Maine), as well as the First Parish Unitarian

Universalist in Concord (Massachusetts), the First Parish in Lexington (Massachusetts), First Parish Universalist Unitarian Church in Waltham (Massachusetts), Ferry Beach Park Association, and countless other congregations, camps, and conference centers that have allowed me over the years to "teach" them about prayer. Each of the classes and workshops I was able to offer was an opportunity for me to learn much.

Of all my teachers and mentors I would single out the Reverend Nancy Rockwell who taught me so much about public praying during my year of student ministry. Hers remain among the most poetic and evocative public prayers I have ever heard. I am deeply in her debt.

It is with great humility that I thank the people at Skinner House Books who, before my first book had even hit the shelves were willing to talk with me about a second and who, again, have helped turn my best attempt at expressing my thoughts into a finished book.

Finally, yet far from least, two familial notes of gratitude: to my mother-in-law, the Reverend Barbara Brand-James, and grandmother-in-law, Mrs. Dena Brand—thank you for all of your tremendous practical and emotional support. And to my wife and best friend, Mary Brand-James, and our two incredible children, Theo and Lester—you are all the proof I need that prayers can be answered, and a constant reminder to give thanks every day.